HOW TO BUILD:
A HOUSE,
A LIFE,
A FUTURE

*How
to Build:
a House,
a Life,
a Future*

Ariane Roesch

Atmen Press

ISBN:
Limited Edition Hardcover: 978-1-7330545-1-5
Hardcover: 978-1-7330545-0-8
Paperback: 978-1-7330545-2-2
Ebook: 978-1-7330545-3-9

Main Chapter Illustrations by Kati Ozanic
Spot Illustrations by Ariane Roesch
Book design by Bruno Pieroni
Edited by Nancy Zastudil

Printed and bound in the USA
First printing September 2019

Published by Atmen Press
Houston, TX USA 77091
Visit www.atmenpress.com

FUNDED IN PART BY THE
CITY OF HOUSTON
THROUGH HOUSTON ARTS ALLIANCE

For Zachary Miano

Table of Contents

Introduction

Throughout my life and career as an artist, Houston, Texas, has been a place of creative risk-taking and possibility. Its no zoning policy mixed with a pervasive do-it-yourself attitude define it as the City of Opportunity. In the midst of a national housing shortage, and with Houston still rebuilding after Hurricane Harvey, my goal was to create a book that inspires people to build.

This book is about building a house—your very own home. It goes beyond unraveling financials and what construction materials are best to use and digs deeper into why building might be your best option. It is a meditation on affordable housing, the student loan crisis, and what happens when a generation can't afford to invest in their community.

As of December 2016, my now-husband Zak and I successfully completed the construction of our home. We were the general contractors who managed or assisted in nearly all aspects of the construction. What had seemed like a straightforward (albeit, stressful) venture turned into a complicated and emotional journey. We navigated hurdles such as new regulations about water mitigation and detention as the city strained to deal with its increasing flood problem. We encountered financial roadblocks related to student debt, lack of steady employment, and inadequate income history.

To make the venture financially feasible, we moved into a 20 ft. shipping container on our property without electricity, water, sewer, or even a fence. We received our building permit eight months later and, over the course of two years, built our new life, slowly regaining standard comforts such as running water and continuous electricity. Ultimately, I realized the most difficult part of living the life you want is not giving up the life you have.

I designed this book to provide information and motivation. I'm not giving any professional advice. Although I've made every effort to ensure that the information in this book was correct at the time it was published, I am not responsible for any physical, psychological, emotional, or financial damages. We are all responsible for our own choices, actions, and results.

This account, as I remember it, is based solely on Zak's and my experiences. We did things the way we did because that's what we knew at the time. We were already off to a good start by having a lively group of family members, friends, and acquaintances who had either built houses or worked in the industry but we finished our journey gaining many more. Although some people might not be mentioned here or their names have been changed to protect their privacy, I certainly have a new found appreciation and utmost respect for everyone who was along for the ride—for what they do, their knowledge, and their readiness to help despite any financial gain. You know who you are and I thank you.

Our home ended up having a small footprint but, in a way, this book is not about scale or about Zak and me—it is about a general shared economic viability and awareness. How much do we need versus what do we want versus how much can we actually afford? It's about living within our means and within our desires.

This is a story of how to build: a house, a life, a future.

CHAPTER ONE

Finding Land

O ur home journey started in 2012. Zak and I were living in an old bungalow in the Heights area of Houston with our two dogs, Abbie and Zarro. The rent was fair, we had a decent-sized yard, and the location was good for us. I could walk the dogs through the neighborhood to the park almost everyday. It had a circular track and a baseball field just off to the side. If we were alone, I would let them off the leash to run around the red, sandy diamond.

I had just moved back from Los Angeles after receiving a Master of Fine Arts from the California Institute of the Arts. Zak, who was working as a merchant marine, and I met two weeks before I left for school and miraculously stayed together during those two years. It was the first time I had lived away from family and friends, really anybody that I knew. Our relationship grew through phone and online conversations, providing a lifeline as our lives unfolded in separate parts of the world.

The bungalow we settled into was 888 sq. ft. with two bedrooms, one bathroom, and two porches, situated in the middle of a 5,000 sq. ft. lot. To say "two bedrooms" is generous, considering that the second room, my studio/guest bedroom, was more like a walk-in closet (it barely fit a twin bed and desk). Our bedroom was spacious with large windows overlooking the yard. Both the bedroom and living room had high, vaulted ceilings that dropped to 8 ft. in the dining room. The dining room had a low, excessively structured ceiling—thick paint globs protruded into the room making it feel even more like a cave. In the kitchen, the ceiling wasn't the only thing that dropped. The floor also slanted toward the back of the house, its tile enhancing a fun house-like feeling. The small bathroom behind the kitchen seemed like it was about to sink into the ground.

Everybody found the house charming, including the roaches and rodents. Within a month of living there, we had sealed all the cracks under the cabinets and along the floorboards and installed mesh along the underside of the house where we noticed large holes. But all of our pest-prevention didn't do much; afterall, we did live in Houston and cockroaches are just part of everyday life. The large native tree roaches (that can also fly!) live in the underbrush and more or less stumble inside a house rather than invade it from the inside. The rodents were a bit more disturbing. I remember one night, while reading at the dining table, hearing a rustling sound. After inspecting all the known trouble spots, I carefully bent over the burners to inspect the back of the stove; I saw a mouse sitting on the pipes. Apparently the whole family had moved in and was living behind the stove during the winter to keep warm. I finally called pest control but the guy just walked me around the house, shaking his head, pointing out the giant holes all over the walls just under the roof line. I could then see the black smudges around the openings—rubbings from the animals' fur as they made their way in and out of our house.

Since we had a yard and porches, we started to garden but kept all the plants in five-gallon buckets with handles. We had two sage trees on either side of the stairs leading to the front porch, two jasmine trees that flanked the porch posts, and our first rose bush, all ready to be picked up and carried away at any point.

We never planned on being in that house very long so, when our two-year lease came up for renewal, we started looking at other options. Maybe something that didn't have holes or pests living in the attic? Maybe a place with central air conditioning and heat? I was twenty-nine years old and felt like these things should be attainable.

We started by searching the Houston Association of Realtors (HAR) database online, a real estate website for the Houston area. Having been frustrated with the cosmetic state of the bungalow, we entertained the idea of purchasing something, perhaps something we could fix up, something that could be an investment. But the house-hunting process proved to be disheartening. I made a list of properties in our price range that we wanted to see in person. We met our realtor at each house with our hopes high only to have them sink with every step toward the front door: small front

yards, low ceilings, dark rooms, tile floors, and barely
any breathing space between the driveway and the
neighbor's house.[1]

We did find one house that I fell in love with. Priced
at $80,000, it was a one-story with three bedrooms
and two bathrooms, a nice-sized yard, and centrally
located near the city's future METROrail expansion.
It was similar to our rental house but in much better
shape and, at 1,200 sq. ft., a little bit bigger. As I was
envisioning the future renovations, Zak was walking
around the house, kneeling on the ground inspecting the
underbelly. The nextdoor neighbor came out and chatted
us up across the 4 ft. tall chain link fence separating the two
yards. We felt good about the place and the location, so I started
getting paperwork in order to put in an offer. I felt so proud of our home
buying efficiency.

In the end, we didn't get the house. Someone else put in a higher offer and
the owners accepted it. We didn't realize that 2012 was just the beginning of
Houston's hot real estate market following the 2008 Great Recession.[2] I'm
not sure how many hands the house has passed through since our attempt
at purchasing it but it sold in 2016 for $184,000. The pictures online revealed
a new paint job, a red door, and kitchen remodel. But I could still see the
cracked brick and mortar steps that lead to the backyard and the chain link
fence still leans just so.

Ed Hardy

In June 2012, tattoo artist Don Ed Hardy had an exhibition at The Art
Guys' studio located in a neighborhood called Acres Homes on the northside
of Houston. The Art Guys were a local collaborative artist duo and I had
gotten a glimpse of their new space when they held an open house for
their newly self-built studio and home. I recall driving with my mother
to the event, feeling like we were driving to the deep woods of Houston. I
had never even seen or heard of this part of Houston and was pleasantly
surprised when we got there: a long, winding driveway led to a metal house
in the woods with horses grazing across the street. I remembered the trees
and open space most from that first trip, and it was those same trees that
welcomed Zak and me in 2012 when we arrived to see Hardy's show. As we
stood outside the studio, enjoying a beer in the stillness of an early summer

evening, we agreed that this is what we were looking for: trees, open space, a house with a studio located away from the main street. We wanted a house in the woods, we wanted quiet. We wanted it to be our own. After that night, things came into focus. We weren't searching for a house, we were searching for land.

Paradise

I had been looking regularly for available lots, keeping an eye on anything in and around Acres Homes, when I saw the following listing in the spring of 2013 on the HAR website: "Paradise Lane. $20,000. ½ acre." I was immediately intrigued. Sight unseen, I fell in love. Zak remembers coming home to me excitedly telling him about what I had found and that I wanted to live in Paradise, accentuating the definitive statement with a stomp of my foot. And that was that.

Acres Homes is a neighborhood with strong rural roots. People ride their horses down the street, sometimes bareback with just a rope to lead or fully-decked out in Western gear, the horses proudly prancing down streets named after William Wilberforce and Phillis Wheatley. It is probably also the only place in Houston to see a donkey-drawn carriage with rims, making its way through the neighborhood, blasting hip-hop, soul, and RnB tunes. Before 1967, Acres Homes was considered the largest unincorporated African American community in the Southern United States. Land was sold by the acre for farm animals and gardens. To this day, families own large areas of land that have been passed down through generations.

Paradise is only two blocks long. Horses graze across the street from an elementary school playground. One-story single family houses sparingly dot either side of the street. Although each yard is fenced, the gates are open and the front yards are kept trim and clean. It is a quiet neighborhood street. We stopped in front of the property. The full depth of 334 feet was littered with tall trees and shrubs, showing no sign of human intervention. It was perfect.

Jim

Jim is one of those amazing old guys Zak has known since he was a little boy. Zak's late father, sculptor Mik Miano, and Jim were close, skating alongside each other as members of the Urban Animals, a 1980s Houston inner-city roller skating tribe. They worked together on special effects for movies (like *Robocop II* which was filmed in Houston), sculptures, and art cars. With piercing blue eyes peering over wire-rimmed bifocals, a belly-length dreaded beard, unkempt hair, and occasionally wearing a kilt with work boots, Jim is quite a sight. A carpenter and Jack-of-all-trades, his demeanor is more like that of a pirate. He could probably set anything on fire. The booming housing industry of the early 1980s brought him to Houston and he stayed as it developed into more than just an oil town.

The first time I met Jim was at a bar. He had just finished installing the new women's bathroom stalls. A couple of whiskeys and who knows how many beers later, he was celebrating a job well done and wanted to show me his completed project. He walked me into the bathroom, adding that it also had great acoustics. Standing just inside the women's bathroom, looking at a pair of beautifully crafted wooden stalls, Jim put his arm around me and started singing a Willie Nelson song, drawing out the "o's" to catch the perfect pitch.

Back in 2012, while we were looking at houses and had our property epiphany, Jim happened to sell his warehouse. The neighborhood was changing and he couldn't afford to stay there so decided to cash in. Not having much of a plan—the sale happened quicker than expected—he ended up living in his box truck, waiting to see what opportunities would present themselves. At this juncture, Zak approached Jim with a proposition, asking for a loan to buy land and in turn we would help Jim find his own piece of property to build a house of his own. "If you're going to live the way you're living, you might as well be on your own property!" were Zak's exact words. Jim was intrigued. He added the stipulation that he would like his and our properties to be next door to or at least down the street from each other; even better, we could build both houses at the same time. And so began our collective search for land. Together, they set out to investigate the neighborhoods and lots that I mapped out.

The Paradise lot did end up being perfect. They stopped the car and walked the total depth of the property, into the woods away from the street. They saw the amazing trees, the wildlife, and relished the peace and quiet.

There was one acre for Jim and, just a few lots down, a half-acre for Zak and me.

The sale went through without problems for Jim; he bought his land with cash and then it was our turn. Unfortunately, the owners of the property we had our eyes on wanted us to give up our mineral rights. We didn't even know what that meant but we figured if we were going to buy land, all of it should be included, even the ground deep below the surface. Luckily, there was another half-acre for sale further down the street. We put in an offer and once again we hit a roadblock—there were problems with the deed. Apparently the person who had leased-to-own the lot died and now the deed was in limbo. We became more and more discouraged.

Meanwhile, Jim started putting up a fence to secure his perimeter; Zak helped when he had time. We were in the thick of August, the heat of summer, and they drove each fence pole by hand into the dry gumbo dirt characteristic of Houston. One day, as they were working, a tractor came by and started filling in and cleaning up the property right next to Jim's. They stopped the worker and asked him what was happening. He told them the property was going to be put up for sale. Serendipitously, the same realtor who sold the property to Jim was handling this sale. Zak and I called and put in an offer on the property before it ever hit the market.

Accepting the Offer

Zak and I found ourselves in a small room with beige walls. The heavy, dark, maple wood and leather furniture seemed too big, too impressive. We had to squeeze behind the plush swivel chairs surrounding the austere conference table to get to our seats. A lonely glass jar filled with candy sitting in the middle of the giant table was the only pop of color. A few framed posters but not much else adorned the walls. Some taxidermied bucks would have completed the picture nicely.

The room felt like stepping back into 1980s boomtown Houston, complete with the couple selling us the property: the Johnsons. His hair was thin, gelled, and slicked back. He wore a casual sport coat and jeans with a thick belt buckle. The appropriate gold class rings adorned his fingers. She wore a bedazzled jean jacket, with thick teased curls cascading around the collar. Her bangs were a single wave crashing on her forehead. She also had rings on her fingers, bangles on her wrist, layered long necklaces, and sparkling earrings that matched everything. Her makeup was thick, heavy on the pink side, with rosy cheeks.

This is where we signed paperwork for our property. I don't know if it was the situation or the decoration but it all felt so grown up. It seemed wrong to reach for the candy. We were about to spend $22,500 on land—more money than either of us had ever spent on anything, money we borrowed yet we didn't even know how the house was going to come to fruition.

We sat around the table, awkwardly waiting for the mass of paperwork to be printed, occasionally exchanging glances and making small talk. The Johnsons asked what we had planned. "Oh, a house! How nice." They purchased the land years ago as an investment. In the end, it all went smoothly. The title company representative elegantly flipped over the contract pages one by one, like a card trick, separating the various copies. We signed first, then the Johnsons. In the end, we shook hands, said our goodbyes and left. Zak and I—two individuals with right to survivorship—were now proud land owners.

CHAPTER TWO

Why Build?

Shelter is a basic need that, as humans, has to be met for our physical and psychological well-being. In 2017, close to 800,000 single family houses were completed in the United States.[3] So why build?

My grandmother said she built her house in post-WWII Germany because she didn't want to live in a house that had belonged to someone else; she wanted *her* house. She also didn't want to deal with landlords or rising rents. She and my grandfather found a plot of land on a hill on the outskirts of a sought after suburb of Frankfurt and planned to build one of three houses that overlooked the town. They, along with a newborn (my mom), lived in a one-room apartment rental for two years while building their house. My grandfather drew the plans and did most of the engineering. Saving money from each paycheck, buying what they could and not borrowing any money, they slowly built the house. When they moved in, the exterior was built but only the kitchen, bathroom, and one bedroom were finished. The remaining rooms were still under construction for another two years.

Not only were they able to get exactly what they wanted in terms of floor plan and renovate the house as the needs for their growing family changed, but building their own house also allowed them to do it piece-by-piece; essentially, they were able to finish the house without ever needing a mortgage. These days, my grandmother can't believe it when people say they can't afford to build a house. If they could pull it off in post-WWII Germany, then it could be done anywhere, right?

Not quite. Despite the tragedy and rubble that Germany was reduced to post-WWII, it was experiencing a "Wirtschaftswunder" by the mid-1950s. The currency was reformed in 1948 to the more stable Deutsche Mark, the social market economic system had taken hold, and optimism abounded. Goods and labor were valued once more.[4] Although much can be said about economic reform as the main driver for this optimism, the incredible

willpower of the German people can't be overlooked. Humiliated, destroyed, having lost everything—homes, family members, possessions, etc.—they still maintained their will to live and forge a way to rebuild their homes and their country.

This post-war boom spread all across the Western world, heralding the "Golden Age of Capitalism." New products hit the market as salaries steadily increased, promising everyone a shot at the good life. In the 1950s in the United States, the average annual income for a family was $3,300.[5] A car cost $1,510 and a house $7,354, or 45 percent and 222 percent of a family's annual income, respectively.[6] Tuition at a reputable university was between $600 to $800 (18 to 20 percent) per year.[7] The American Dream was in full swing. Everyone was keeping up with the Jones' and home ownership was at an all-time high of 55 percent.[8]

Fast forward to 2013. The subprime housing crisis that led to the Great Recession in 2008 had finally recovered. The average annual family income was $52,250 but to buy a car that family had to spend an average of $31,252 (60 percent).[9,10] On average, a house could set them back $324,500 (620 percent).[11] School tuition was now $8,893 (17 percent) per year for a public four-year in-state college.[12] A private university could be as much as $30,094 (57 percent) per year.[13]

The cost of living has increased dramatically in the last sixty years along with an ever-widening pay gap. The middle class is dwindling and most people don't have the savings to cover a $400 emergency.[14] Jobs with steadily advancing income are being replaced by a growing "gig economy."[15]

So why build your own house? It has become more difficult to build since the 1950s, with tougher regulations in place. As new housing—even affordable housing—is being constructed, it may seem like an unnecessary pursuit. But it might just be a revolutionary response to some of the problems facing our society today.

First, you get what you want within the parameters of what you can afford; you have quality and budget control. You set the priorities and, in the end, the house is a reflection of who you are. Cities have become more like cornfields—efficient but without complexity. And yet it is this complexity, this diversity, that is necessary for a thriving and lively city.[16] This kind of character can't be planned for or orchestrated; it comes from the many individuals who inhabit a place.

Building your own house also produces an awareness of the intricacies of life; it's an exercise in civic awareness, what constitutes shelter, a review of necessities, and an investigation in quality. Increasingly there is a societal focus on productivity and using our time in the most efficient way, where "efficiency" is just another word for speed. I believe anyone can build their own house if they are able to sacrifice their time and be inefficient, allowing for mistakes and space to contemplate and fix them. Building your own house is the antithesis of what society demands from us.

Ownership can encourage people to become more involved in their community. They have skin in the game. They want to live in a good neighborhood and still be able to afford it. How is city policy affecting the community? What is happening at the school down the street? How is the neighbor's concrete bungalow impacting flood levels? How could development affect the immediate ecosystem?

Real estate is still the best long-term investment and equity builder, and therefore it is a wealth creator. Financial net worth has, unfortunately, become the unit of measurement of an individual's worth. As with any industry, real estate is about money and the ever-churning over of properties, continuously squeezing out profits and raising values. Building your own home stabilizes the market due to the house never being publicly bought or sold; it removes the financial speculation. It may be the antidote to this arbitrary system.

I'm not advocating for a back-to-the-land-type movement but rather a move back to the self, reinvigorating neighborhoods with a self-sufficiency and character that will reignite the complex fabric from which our cities grew.

And wouldn't it be better if we all were a little bit more engaged?

CHAPTER THREE

Living Situation

We signed our purchase contract for the Paradise property on August 5, 2013. As soon as the contract was finalized, we gave notice to our landlord: We were moving out! And moving on up. Or so we thought.

The Carriage House

Through a friend, we found a seemingly sweet situation. A landlord needed tenants for the smaller carriage house on one of his properties at a cheap rate. It was in walking distance to a large park and museums. The layout was a little weird but we could live with it since our stay was temporary. We should have seen the red flags waving big and bright within the first week of staying there but we needed a place to live.

The backstory was that someone had broken into the complex to steal the copper from the air conditioning units. In order for the insurance company to pay the claim, the owner needed to prove he had tenants living there. We went along with it; he helped us and we helped him. We were happy to keep an eye on things. What we didn't find out until later was that he also needed to have someone stay in the main house. So, he concocted a "recently divorced bachelor" who traveled a lot for business and had been renting the main house.

Although we were pretty self-contained in the carriage house, the laundry room was in the main house. We had to walk through the sprawling, beautiful, old house, carrying our laundry, careful not to disturb the set that had been created to tell the story of "recently divorced bachelor." Toothpaste was smeared just so in the sink; an air mattress with messy sheets and a comforter was laid on the floor; newspapers were piled on a table with a dirty coffee mug next to them (there might have even been coffee stains on the paper); a pair of shoes, some shirts, ties, and pants hung in a closet and half-eaten packages of food were in the fridge. It really was believable and would have made a great set for a murder mystery, especially at night when the light from the street lamps illuminated the rooms, throwing long shadows from the grid structures of the country-style windows.

Although we were located in a nice upscale neighborhood and had an electric rolling gate securing the property, we didn't feel safe. The whole situation was awkward. Our two dogs had to stay sequestered inside even though there was a yard, just in case someone needed to see the spectacle happening in the main house. Also, nothing seemed to work correctly in the carriage house. The dishwasher, a luxury we had been looking forward to, didn't work. The house had electric central air and heat but both would shut off after a while and only the fan would run. We had some cold nights that spring and instead of the heater keeping us warm, it would shut off and blow cold air into the already cold room. When it finally warmed up, our bedroom upstairs became the center of hot, stagnant air since all the windows were painted shut. After the first month of living there, we received a $300 utility bill. The electricity probably wasn't separately metered between the two places as the landlord had led us to believe. How could we be saving for a house of our own when we were paying that much for just electricity?

Not only were we sequestered inside the carriage house, we also did not have a comfortable home. We really missed our little bungalow with the big yard and slanted floor. Even though we now owned land, our dream of building seemed to be going nowhere. We felt stuck. Nothing seemed to be moving forward.

To lift our spirits, we spent our weekends on our property which was undeveloped, unmanicured, undesired, and unmaintained. It was covered with large, mature trees such as hackberries, oaks, and pines, towering 60 to 80 ft. above us. Weeds grew wild as did spring onions, morning glories, and blackberries. An assortment of birds traversed the sky and it seemed that the natural ecosystem was still in good order. The dogs could play and   run around at last. We planted some of the potted plants we brought from our little bungalow and envisioned a life that seemed within reach. It was just so peaceful.

Before we moved, Yolle, a friend who had initially introduced Zak and me, needed to unload a couple of 40 ft. shipping containers. He was selling some of his property that he was mainly using for storage, so he approached Zak and Jim, since we now had the land to put them on, to take the containers. We were moving out and needed storage on the property, especially for tools once construction started—it was a no-brainer. We called a wrecker service and the two containers made their way to our side of town. There was some brief discussion about placement but we eventually decided to place our container towards the front, parallel to our property line, and put Jim's further inside the property just past where the future driveway would be, parallel to the street. As we started spending more time on our property, we carved out a little space for ourselves in the container so we could extend our visits.

By this time it was early 2014. It had been so cold and we weren't able to heat up our carriage house rental with the system in place and had to use a propane heater indoors. Since that worked well to warm up the downstairs living room, we started sleeping on our couch futon and not using our bedroom. Even though we weren't using the heating system, the electric bill did not reflect that. It was higher than previously and I couldn't take it anymore: the pretend tenant next door, the over-protectiveness of the dogs, and the various appliances not working. That was it.

I called our previous realtor and said we were back in the saddle, looking for a place to live and needing something quickly. I put together a list of apartments we were interested in and off we went. I spent a day looking and taking pictures. It was all just so sad. Houston had experienced a housing boom starting in 2013 with almost 1,000 people arriving every week.[17] The trend was still going strong in 2014 and it was difficult to find anything in our price range. The places we looked at and could afford at around $1,000 per month were small, dark, did not have a yard, windows were painted shut, with doors that didn't lock. (In comparison, the bungalow was $850 per month.) Nothing was right. We had spent the past year dreaming about owning something and, even though we now had the perfect plot of land, we had not made it past the planning stages.

Jim completed his fence and bought a trailer to camp on the grounds. He was happy living out there. And who could blame him—he was camping in the middle of the city! Frustrated, stressed, and at a loss for options, I told my mom that maybe Zak and I should just buy a trailer and camp as well. And she replied, to my surprise, "Why not?" Yes, why not?

I had always dreamed about living in a trailer. I told Zak about it on our first date. He dreamed of building his own house and I wanted to live in a trailer in the desert (well, maybe a little more than a trailer, more like a doublewide). I love the efficiency of the ready-made, assembled on delivery, with built-in storage for everything. Pick your land and have homeownership delivered for a fair price. I love the tiny house movement. I love the idea of people living with less, making do with what they have.

In a way, our situation meant I could realize my dream of living in a trailer, not really in the desert but on one-half acre of wooded land in North Houston. But purchasing a nice trailer meant we would need a considerable chunk of money up front. Instead, we looked at the container sitting on our property as a possible option.

We couldn't live in the 40 ft. container since we were still using it as our storage unit and tool shed. But what about getting a smaller 20 ft. container, add windows, and position it in the back of our property for privacy? I ran the budget and, for $2,000, which would have been equal to a deposit of first and last month's rent for an apartment, we could get a container delivered.[18] We drew up a quick estimate for wood studs, insulation, some cabinets for a little kitchen, and figured in another $1,000 to $1,500 to get it ready to live in. We spent our nights researching camping gear and how to live without electricity, water, or a sewer system. There were camping toilets, water dispensers, and solar-powered cell phone battery chargers. We would need a generator for a small air conditioner and coolers for food. Most importantly, we learned it was possible. This would be the most affordable route for us and it would be new and it would be ours.

Decision made, Zak went down by the ship channel to choose a container and have it delivered. He selected a beautiful baby blue container. In the meantime, I drew up some possible floor plans to determine where we would place our furniture and other vital belongings and, more importantly, to decide where we would put the door and windows. I taped off the area of the container in our living room at the carriage house and rearranged our furniture to see how, in actuality, we could live in a box that was 8 ft. wide. It seemed a bit daunting but doable to realize how much our surroundings would shrink. It was exciting and definitely scary. This was our first attempt at making a home on our land and felt very much like a precursor to building our house—a trial run without consequences. We negotiated layout, window placement, and had a strict budget. If it didn't work, we could always rejoin civilization and rent one of those crappy apartments.

The Container

We gave our one-month notice to the carriage house landlord and got to work. Zak knew how to weld so he cut out the openings for windows and doors, built an interior framework of 2 x 4 in. studs, inserted insulation, and installed drywall. I picked out paint colors and packed away our things, planning out the next few months. Essentials went into the small container, not-so-essentials into the big container, and non-essentials into a newly rented storage unit. We needed to clear space in the big container for a shop area. It felt good to know we were now going home, and our final move would be into the house we built.

For some people, this solution was completely nuts but, in a strange way, I felt like the experience could be a digital detox or cleansing for me. I daydreamed about reading a book in the hammock as the trees swayed with the wind, taking care of a garden, playing chess, eating by candlelight, recycling water, and just being conscious about what we waste. In other words, being able to relax because some of the worries of civilized life would be gone. Most importantly this eliminated a rent payment (which would have been a minimum of $1,000 per month); instead, we could use that money to invest in something we owned.

Moving Day

We labeled boxes with either a "C" for container or "S" for storage. C items were loaded into the truck first and S items went in last since that would be our first stop. With the help of friends, things went pretty smoothly. When they went to unload at the storage unit, I stayed behind to clean the carriage house and make sure we didn't miss anything. I took a quick shower and realized that I should probably savor the moment since it would be a while before I could just "hop in the shower" again.

Our little storage unit was not climate controlled. When I first looked at it, I was a bit shocked. It was an 8 x 10 x 8 ft. plywood box with a big, black roach poison trap. But it was affordable and that was what really mattered. We deposited all of our things: our bed, books, records, electronics, tables, chairs, lamps, artwork, etc., to someday see again.

When we got to our property, we unloaded our futon bed, a side table, two chairs, four plastic bins of clothes and bed sheets, towels, toiletries, a candelabra along with all the candles we had, essential kitchen and food supplies, and the bowls and bed for our two dogs. We had our camping toilet set-up, a propane camper stove, a cooler full of drinking water, and some five-gallon jugs with non-potable water.

We finished unloading everything into the container before the sun started going down. We set up a little water station outside, along with coolers of food. I put clean sheets on the bed. It was dark; we had our little battery-operated LED light but not much more. We were so exhausted and just wanted to sleep but needed to wash off the sweat and mosquito spray from the day. We boiled some water on our stove to make a batch of warm water for bathing. In the darkness, among the trees swaying in the wind, we stripped down and washed off in a 30-gallon plastic trash can, pouring water over each other. After drying off, we closed the container doors, opened all the windows, and slept peacefully and comfortably for the first time in months.

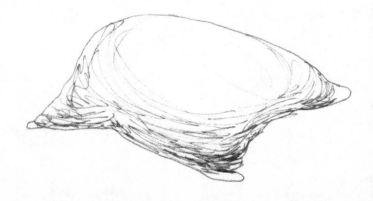

CHAPTER FOUR

What is a Homestead?

The word "homestead" has romantic appeal. It is defined as a lifestyle of self-sufficiency, independence, and living off the land, but the specifics that define something as livable can change depending on the city or county in which the land is located. Houston is interesting in that it does not implement citywide zoning laws. "No zoning" refers to the City of Houston's light regulation of land use and real estate developments.[19] Unless there are neighborhood deed restrictions, it isn't unusual to see an auto mechanic shop next to a row of single family houses. Typically, in cities with zoning ordinances, auto mechanic shops are classified as commercial or industrial and are kept away from the residential areas. Commercial and residential are interwoven through this sprawling city. If you purchased the land, it is yours to do with whatever you wish. For example, on our block there are residential single family homes, an elementary school, grazing horses, and a construction company.

When Zak and I started thinking about our future home, we kept a running list of desired features, things we had seen at other houses we liked, which included the following:

- Open floor plan, simple layout, modern look
- Concrete slab foundation
- High ceilings
- Lots of natural light
- No stairs upon entry
- Live/work situation (a must have)
- Wide porches to enjoy nature
- Big double sink in front of a kitchen window
- Spacious bathroom with big tub

Since we wanted this to happen quickly and efficiently, we researched various ways of getting a shelter in place as soon as possible. There were a few options:

Prefabricated Houses: There are an assortment of companies designing "prefab" houses that aren't the standard double-wide trailer. The models are modern, made with sustainable materials, energy efficient, and delivered as pre-manufactured parts installed on site. The companies usually have a predetermined number of floor plans to choose from, depending on desired square footage, and most are full service so they will handle design, engineering, permitting, building, and lender finalization. Once a buyer selects the design, the process is pretty much on autopilot.

House Moving: Rather than demolish old houses to build something new, some companies specialize in structural relocation, raising houses off their foundations and driving them away. Usually, these houses are built on piers so it is easy to gain access and raise them, moving them to or from a plot of land. The companies normally specialize within a city and are familiar with the building codes to guide buyers through the permitting process once the house is on the property.

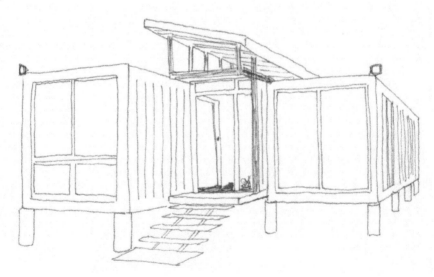

Container Houses: We were also interested in container homes, obviously. Two or three 40 ft. shipping containers can be arranged as structural anchors for a home, complete with a common space in the middle. This is a flexible layout solution and, with enough space, can be easily expanded or altered.

Industrial Metal Buildings: There are also companies that assemble industrial metal buildings in various standard sizes, such as 40 x 60 ft. or 20 x 30 ft. Once a concrete slab foundation is poured, a crew is sent out to erect a steel I-Beam skeleton over which corrugated metal is attached. The structure will include windows, doors (roll-up and standard), insulation, and gutters, engineered to withstand heavy rains and hurricane-force winds.

Both the container and industrial building ideas were interesting since we envisioned that we would erect a shell, something that was finished on the outside with just the bare essentials on the inside, and get it approved by the city. We could then take our time to putz around on the inside, building it out or adding things as needed, or so we thought.

Once we had a city-approved dwelling, we could apply to be a homestead—not very romantic but legally and financially beneficial. Texas has one of the broadest homestead protections in the U.S. which exempts a homestead from forced sale for collection of debt, except for a mortgage or liens.[20] Essentially, someone could only lose their home due to death, abandonment, sale, or foreclosure. The city evaluates property and assigns a taxable and market value. Property taxes in Texas are determined by the taxable value of the home, minus the deductions the homestead exemption provides: a $25,000 reduction on the home's taxable value for public school taxes plus up to an additional 20 percent off on other taxing units within the City of Houston. Also, the home's taxable value increase is locked in at a maximum of 10 percent per year.[21,22]

The only provision to getting a property homesteaded—and receive all these benefits—is it has to be a primary, inhabited residence; living in a tent or a shipping container without utilities won't cut it. Whatever structure is used as a primary residence has to be legally sited on the property. These provisions are set forth in the City of Houston's Code of Ordinances.[23] Since there are no zoning regulations, these ordinances cover a lot of ground, literally. Everything from sidewalks, to parking lots, to drilling for oil is outlined. In terms of building and city planning, city codes are an exercise in minimum standards and are worth a look when thinking about building.

According to the overcrowding definition, the minimum net square footage required for shelter is 150 sq. ft. for one person, plus a minimum of 100 sq. ft. for each additional occupant.[24] For two people that means 250 sq. ft. Within that space there needs to be at least one habitable (meaning used for living, sleeping, eating, or cooking) room that has a floor area of 120 sq. ft. These habitable rooms also can't be less than 7 ft. in any direction (except kitchens) and the minimum ceiling height is 7 ft. tall.

It's interesting to think about our 20 ft. shipping container—it essentially satisfies these requirements in terms of square footage for one person. It has a ceiling height of 8 ft. and is 8 ft. wide. With a total of 160 sq. ft. available, it could have a 120 sq. ft. "main" room with a 40 sq. ft. bathroom and kitchenette. It is humbling to think in terms of minimums when building. The options were endless regarding what our home could be. But how much did we really need?

CHAPTER FIVE

Your Worth

Before purchasing our land, we attended a home buyer class offered by an organization in Houston called Avenue CDC which assists low-income families apply for housing grants from the city. The class was a prerequisite for the grant and covered all the essentials including credit, budgeting, and types of mortgages. We learned we could qualify for a $30,000 grant from the city if we lived in the house for ten years. Even if you do not qualify for low-income housing or are looking to buy a home, a class like this can be helpful.

As is the case with many of these weekend classes, the lessons were presented like a stand-up comedy routine. The teacher was wonderful. Animated and charismatic, he told funny anecdotes from his home buying ventures, sometimes taking stabs at the quirks of family life in a prime-time television sort of way. This class was quite the marathon, 8:00 a.m. to 4:00 p.m. on a Saturday, but he stayed upbeat and never broke character.

Although the morning was filled with many valuable points—such as how an online media subscription saves hundreds of dollars on family movie nights, and that whirlpool tubs are a waste of water and electricity and should not be a selling point—we walked away with one important lesson: how to distribute debt as a couple. Even if a couple is married, it all depends on whose signature is on the documents (useful information that would come in handy later on). For example, when buying a house, one partner can sign for the house which frees up the other person to take on an additional loan if needed (a car loan, for example). We decided that I would take on the house loan, even though I had student loans, since I had a steady job working with my mom full-time and a good credit history, while Zak had the know-how to build the house and could act as the general contractor. It was the only way to make it work.

We were really hoping to qualify for one of the city grants as a low-income couple, which meant a maximum average median income of $42,400 for two people in 2013, but unfortunately this doesn't apply to construction loans to build your own home.[25] In any case, we were armed with a better understanding of the path-to-equity process and all the pieces that went into it.

As I approached bankers and lenders for construction loan info, I found them to be very positive at first, saying things like, "Of course, this is a great idea!" and "Sure, we can make this happen!" But once we sent the stack of requested paperwork, they said I didn't qualify. But how I could qualify was never discussed. Obviously, we were wasting the bankers time with our artsy blueprints, simple budgets, printed online research, etc. Their role wasn't really to invest; they wanted to make absolutely sure they would get their money back.

Candice

I finally reached out to an old friend, Candice, who had been working at a bank for the past few years and was making her way up the corporate ladder. She started as a teller and was now handling lot loans. We met in ninth grade gym class and her sure-fire way of speaking with a steadfast approach to creative problem-solving made us fast friends. I admired her confidence in knowing what she wanted at such a young age.

Over the years since high school, we slowly drifted apart; we stayed in contact but were on different paths. I pursued becoming an artist, getting a Bachelor of Fine Arts in Photo/Digital Media at the University of Houston, applying for shows, making art, organizing exhibitions. I was more focused on building my artist resume than a professional resume. I decided to attend graduate school and moved away. She started with an engineering degree but left UH to work. After a series of jobs, she got an associate degree in finance which landed her at a bank. I lived at home after college, whereas she had moved out after highschool with her then-boyfriend, now husband. They got married, had kids. I just couldn't relate.

It was 2013 and I was happy to reconnect with a confidant to help Zak and me build a house. I remember sitting across from her at her official bank desk. I had two degrees, she had two kids. I was still working for my mom and Candice had her own desk at a bank with two chairs for guests. She had a steady job and I had a closet full of artwork, a lengthy resume, and somewhat of a career.

As she looked over my two years of tax returns and a statement I pulled together of projected income for 2013, she just started shaking her head and bluntly said, "Ariane, you just have to make more money!" Yes, I know. I listed some commissions that were going to come through and she nodded and said great but that I was still nowhere near where I needed to be. And then she did something no one had been able to do up to that point. She took out a piece of paper and explained to me how I would be able to qualify. She started with our projected cost to construct the house and worked backwards. All of a sudden it was like we were back in high school, with her explaining a complicated calculus equation to me. I learned how to calculate my debt-to-income ratio, how mortgage payments factor in, and that W-2 income is always preferred to 1099 income, no matter how many 1099 forms I had. Security, not quantity, is what really counts.

And you know what? I wasn't that far off! What had seemed like a doomed mission all of a sudden became feasible again.

DTI Exercise

A debt-to-income ratio (DTI) is calculated by adding all monthly payment obligations and dividing them by gross (before taxes) monthly income. If you are self-employed, i.e. receive 1099s, the bank will take an average of the last two years of business net income (net = income - expenses) as it is reflected on your tax return. The bank or lender will use the credit report to see debt obligations, such as credit card debt, car loans, or student loans. Even though the maximum or standard repayment amount is listed for student loans, credit card debt will show the minimum payment due. In addition to existing debt, lenders will factor in future mortgage payments, property taxes, and house insurance based on the house you would like to buy or build.

The magic DTI ratio we needed to hit was 43 percent or less, meaning my overall debt had to be 43 percent or less of my monthly gross income.[26] This percentage seems to waver a bit but what lenders are looking for is less than 45 percent debt to income. DTI can be calculated by starting with monthly salary or with the value of the home (a sample exercise can be found in the appendix of this book). Keep in mind that this exercise involves a lot of estimation based on location.

Education

A major piece of my debt-to-income ratio puzzle was my student loan. Debt from my undergraduate and graduate degrees equaled $97,304.17. And I think I'm one of the lucky ones. Some of my classmates who went to private out-of-state schools for their degrees owe more than $200,000. As of 2018, the total amount of national outstanding student debt was $1.5 trillion.[27]

Before deciding to pursue my master's degree, I asked other artists about the amount of debt student loans would create. Their responses were usually nonchalant: "Yeah, I mean, we each have essentially a mortgage," or "Yes, the student loans suck but you can make payments based on your income or even defer them at times when you can't make a payment." It seemed to be more about debt management. Let lenders know if you can't make a payment. Send in new paperwork if your income changes. Just don't stop communicating with lenders or paying something. The artists I talked to discussed the topic with such ease and seemed to still be able to exhibit their art, travel, and have families. So, when it came time to sign the promissory notes, I didn't think twice. Whatever it took. Bring it. I wanted to be an artist and having a master's degree from one of the top schools in the country would not only set me apart but would help further my art practice, my network, and my understanding of what art could be.

When the funds were disbursed, it was like Monopoly money—I never saw any of it, just numbers on a statement. I did get a measly check for the remainder that was supposed to cover my expenses for the semester. I went with my new roommate to pick up our checks at the financial aid office at the beginning of my first semester at the California Institute of the Arts. We stood in a long line that wound down the hallway—all of us getting the bare minimum to live on after the institution was paid. As we got into her car, checks in hand, she turned to me with a sly grin. "Wanna go to Vegas? Double or nothing!" We both had a laugh. It was such an outrageously crazy idea but, in a way, we were already betting on our futures with much slimmer odds.

When Candice pulled my credit report to double-check all the things that needed to be factored into my debt-to-income formula, the student loans had the standard repayment amount listed which hovered just above $1,000 per month. She looked shocked (also at the amount of loans I had) and I calmed her by repeating the nonchalant responses I had been given. "Well, I don't actually pay that. I'm on an income-based repayment plan." And this was when the gravity of the situation sunk in: lenders look at whatever is on your credit report. If I wasn't actually paying $1,000 per month, then I needed to have them change it or provide something in writing that says what I am liable to pay.

This was the start of many conversations with my student loan holders. Between 2013 and 2015, a lot changed to make it easier for people with student loans to apply for a mortgage.[28] During my first phone call, I had to speak to a manager and explain to them what I was trying to do and what the letter addressed to my lender needed to say. The second time, they knew the drill and had a letter already formatted and ready to go. Currently, this is one of the forms available for download from the online portal.

I'm sure I wasn't the only one on an income-based repayment plan trying to apply for a home loan. What happens when a whole generation, weighed down with student debt, trying to continue their lives, is unable to invest in their community? Many of us followed what we thought was the correct path: go to school and get a good education. But even now I can't help but feel like I've done something wrong.

Employment

I have always been active in my family's business. My mother had an art gallery and my father started his own business importing picture frames from Germany after working for years in the oil and gas industry. Around the time in high school when my friends were starting to work, I was getting paid to research galleries and framers online and add their information to a mailing list. When it came time for a big mailing campaign, I recruited friends and we would spend a Saturday at the office stuffing envelopes. I also helped my mother during art exhibition openings. My friends really enjoyed helping with those, since it made for great people watching.

With all the possibilities of the

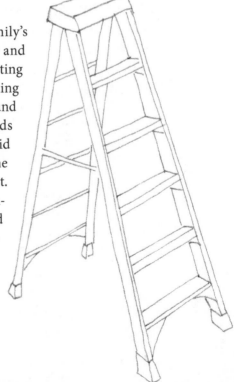

internet at my fingertips, and being fortunate enough to have my own computer, I became interested in creating websites. In the late 1990s and early 2000s, when blogs were just starting, I taught myself HTML and played around with some of the early free website services. A highschool friend and I were all over Angelfire coding GIFs, changing colors, and posting pictures. So when my mom needed a website, I got the job. When my dad was trying to customize his online shopping cart website years later, my knowledge of code came in handy as well.

My father was diagnosed with cancer during my last semester in high school. He was losing weight and not feeling well. Nobody knew what was wrong with him until he fainted in the second floor hallway as he was trying to use the bathroom. I remember rushing down the stairs to find him lying on the floor, looking thin and helpless, with eyes wide in confusion. He was rushed to the emergency room where he underwent tests for weeks until they finally found the small cell cancer in his lung. It had already spread throughout his body and there wasn't much anyone could do for him. My father, whose corporate job had sent his family all over the world and eventually landed us in Houston. My father, who decided to quit corporate life to start an art framing business and build a house, the house that took years to build and he only enjoyed for a few months. My father, who was now fighting for his life, on his final deadline to finish what he started.

I spent the summer after high school helping out in his office, running errands, making sure things were operating smoothly, meeting clients, and fulfilling orders. I was eighteen years old and suddenly found myself managing a company. I learned about QuickBooks, financial statements, logistics, and customer service. With the new house my father built, my mother's art gallery also found a new home and, amid all the health prob-

lems, new art exhibitions were mounted, people were invited, and art was sold.

I applied to begin my undergraduate studies at UH that fall. I wanted some kind of normalcy. The morning my father died, I was in class and received my philosophy test results. I don't remember what my grade was but, as I packed up at the end of class, the weight of everything overwhelmed me and I started to cry. One of the girls sitting close by stopped me on my way out and asked if I was okay. "Did you get a bad grade on your test?" If only.

After he passed, I continued school. When I wasn't in school, I was helping my mother figure out how to make our new situation work. I advanced to learn more about financials and budgeting. Since it was just the two of us, we consolidated everything under one roof. There was an unquestioning confidence we could handle things but I think we both just learned by doing.

What might come as a surprise to other people is that I did not choose business as my undergraduate degree. My mother has had the art gallery since I was seven years old and I think the continuous flow of artists coming to exhibit, discuss, and sell their art had a profound effect on me. They brought a kind of freedom with them, a freedom to engage differently with life, asking questions and not just marching forward in absolutes or adhering to the norms.

Working for a CPA

I had been working closely with our accountant doing basic book-keeping for both of my family's businesses. By the time I turned twenty years old, I was ready for a change. I wanted my own place, my own life. It turned out he was looking for help in his office and so I started working for him part-time while continuing my studies at the university. I learned quickly how to organize receipts, reconcile bank accounts, and prepare personal and business tax returns.

His office was located in an old, beige, four-story building in a busy retail area of Houston. It was a standard commercial space-for-lease building with winding carpeted hallways filled with doorways that could only be distinguished by the little plaques located on the wall next to them. His office was heavy and brown: thick leather chairs, dark wooden desk cabinets, and beige carpet. It had tall ceilings, 12 ft. at least, and consisted of two rooms: a front room or reception area where my desk was and a larger back office with his desk. The overhead fluorescent lights were always on even though one wall of his office was comprised of windows. The long, beige blinds were usually drawn shut, with narrow slits of sunshine coming through. Sometimes, when he wasn't there, I would turn off all the lights and open the blinds as I sorted through receipts.

A large part of my job involved data entry. His clients would send us a box filled with receipts and bank and credit card statements which first

needed to be organized physically and then entered electronically. I found
the reconciliation process exciting. I always loved math and the process
of entering data and seeing that everything balanced, or finding a lonely
transaction that had been overlooked, was fascinating and strangely satis-
fying. It gave me a sense of achievement seeing the numbers fall into their
correct places. I prepared everything either in Excel or QuickBooks and
then transferred the information into an electronic tax report program. He
reviewed everything before finalizing and sending to the IRS.

Although boring and monotonous, in hindsight it was one of the best
opportunities I could have stumbled upon. I learned about finances, deductions, spending habits, and how to organize and submit taxes. And it is true
that people always need help with their accounting—it has paid forward
numerous times. It also laid the foundation to my understanding of the
financial process needed to build a house.

Full-Time

After getting my master's degree, I moved back to Houston and resumed working with my mom at the gallery, primarily helping to import and distribute the German framing product. In the summer of 2014, due to my accounting experience, I started working a few hours a month for an online art magazine. They needed someone to reconcile bank accounts and credit card statements, preparing checks, etc. I had been following this publication for years, reading about the Texas art scene, finding out about calls for art entries, and learning what exhibitions were happening where. I was happy for the extra work. Zak and I had just moved into the 20 ft. shipping container and were in the midst of figuring out how to actually pull off building a house. After I had been working there for a few months, they were in need of a new full-time employee and asked me if I would be interested. Even though this would give me the stable W-2 job I needed, I still had to think about it. I enjoyed my freedom. I liked what I was doing and I was good at it. I had family obligations but the timing seemed too perfect to pass up the opportunity. I had never worked in publishing and didn't really know what I would get myself into. In the end, I jumped on it. It was a crucial piece to our home-building puzzle. I was curious how working for an online company without an internet connection would work out.

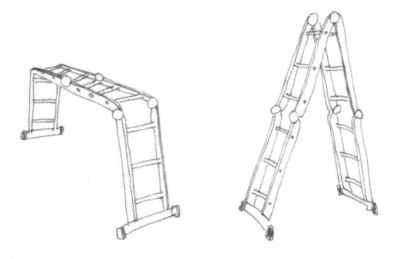

CHAPTER SIX

Container Living

Zak and I lived in our converted 20 ft. shipping container for two-and-a-half years, from May 2014 until October 2016, while planning and building our house. For the first eight months, we didn't have our official building permit which meant we had to live off-the-grid without electricity or proper plumbing. The container still sits on our property and now houses my studio, which is where I'm writing most of this book. It is my box and oddly comforting. I like to recall the simplicity of our time spent living in it. Even though it was small for us at the time, it never felt cramped. Our routine stayed fairly consistent: we cooked almost every night, washed dishes, talked, read, or watched movies (which I downloaded to my computer at work where I had an internet connection). Sometimes we simply sat outside with the dogs and enjoyed the rustling of the towering trees swaying in the breeze.

Our two containers weren't too peculiar for Houston. Thanks to the city's lack of zoning laws, it was not unusual to have a shipping container sitting on a property. In fact, within the immediate streets of our neighborhood, there were several containers, positioned like stoic relics of industry among the overgrown yards with vines slowly enveloping them. I don't think we could have pulled this off in any other major U.S. city. We were surrounded by tall trees even though we were close to downtown; the odd, thin, rectangular shape of the property jutted far away from the street; and the fact that we didn't have any nextdoor neighbors except for Jim, all made this adventure and experiment possible.

Any large commercial construction project usually has an air conditioned mobile home on site as the construction office, we just lived in ours. As we had engineers, surveyors, and similar kinds of people visit the property while building our house, nobody questioned the two shipping containers. If asked, we just said "storage" and that was that. Technically, shipping

containers are considered a temporary structure by the city, unless they
are connected to permanent utilities.

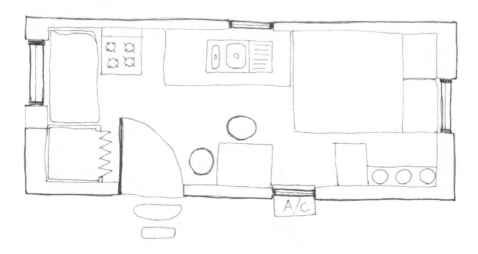

When we first moved to our property in May 2014, we didn't even have
a fence yet—our perimeter was still unsecured. Jim's fence was on one
side but we had yet to close in our remaining three sides which meant we
had some curious night-time visitors during those first few weeks until
everyone got used to us being there. I remember being outside one night at
our water station, brushing my teeth in the low glow of our LED lantern,
when I saw two eyes approaching. A dog's eyes, presumably, since they
reflected a green shimmer in the light. Since we had our dogs with us I did
not immediately freak out, thinking that perhaps it was our black lab mix,
Abbie, approximately the same height. I think I might have even called out
her name, keeping myself calm since I really couldn't see farther than a
few feet in front of me. I only freaked out when the dog finally made it into
the light and I realized it was definitely not Abbie. Thankfully, both of us
were startled to find what we did and left the scene without much further
inquiry. Afterall, Zak and I had encroached on the dog's territory with our
strange metal contraption.

At first, the container was a simple box with just a futon bed, dog bed,
and side table in it. We slowly added a loft area above the bed for storage,
some kitchen cabinets with a sink, a mini-fridge, a folding dining table with
two chairs, a small wardrobe for our clothes, a full-length mirror, a rug, and

an artwork by Texas artist Hills Snyder—a silhouette of Tinkerbell cut out of pink Plexiglass—to keep us company and our hopes afloat.

It was easy to keep tidy; at only 160 sq. ft. we couldn't have much stuff in the first place. There was a lot of sweeping since we had to trek almost 100 ft. through the yard from our cars in the driveway to the container. I always thought of those old Western movies with the standard shot of the prairie woman sweeping the porch of a wooden cabin. But again, the space was so small it was a quick task. It was odd squeezing our lives into one small room. Sometimes, when I woke up, I would look at the door in my half-asleep-state and think it led to another part of the house. Then my eyes would drift to a window and the spell would be broken. Nope, this was it.

More than anything, our time in the container was just inconvenient. It was inconvenient to refill a generator. It was inconvenient to haul our own water. It was inconvenient to put on rain boots to use the bathroom. It was inconvenient to drive to a gym to take a shower. But we could deal with all those inconveniences, especially because we knew it would get better and would eventually end. We just didn't know when.

Before we moved, we acquired some temporary structures left over from the Houston International Festival. Jim helped build several of the structures for the festival over the years and, when it went bankrupt, the city needed to dispose of what was left to avoid paying storage fees for artifacts of festivals gone by. Jim chose things that were close to his heart: a blue and yellow pirate ship built on a trailer, a replica of the towering open-armed Jesus from Brazil he had helped carve, and a replica of a famous Spanish church.

Since we needed some extra cover, we picked the Day of the Dead house. It measured 10 ft. cubed, had a roof, and was perfect as our "bath house." We installed it approximately 15 ft. from our container door and laid bricks in a herringbone pattern for a floor. The bath house contained a large plastic trough, pressurized shower container, composting toilet, hand-washing station, coolers, extra five-gallon water jugs, and various garden tools. There was no door but we had a shower curtain. We used awning scraps to cover the two large window openings to give us privacy while still allowing for airflow. It was not insulated—cold in the winter, sticky in the summer, and swarming with mosquitos and other kinds of bugs. It was a simple bathroom sheltered from the rain, an expanded outhouse.

The Logistics of Living Off the Grid

Electricity

When we first started living in the shipping container, a cool breeze was still in the air. We had our battery-powered electronics, loads of candles, and a positive attitude. We would grill food, make a salad, and eat a romantic candlelit dinner outside. Jim would sometimes join us or we would walk next door and eat there, holding flashlights as we made our way through the weeds in the darkness. And it was so dark. Our container was set roughly 200 ft. away from the street which was illuminated by the street light. We were surrounded by woods; no light made it into our yards except when the moon was full. Sundown meant lights out. After dinner, we might read or watch a movie. Mostly we just went to sleep. Keeping the lights on seemed like a waste of generator fuel.

We discovered the amazing quality of solar lights. We strapped four outdoor solar spot lights on top of the container—one for each corner—and anxiously waited for the sun to set. The effect was out of this world, truly. The four lights beaming at a downward 45 degree angle turned our box into something like a UFO apparition. It must have been a weird sight for anyone driving by, seeing a mysterious illuminated box sitting amongst the weeds. For us, it was perfect because now we could see our immediate surroundings.

We used a workhorse of a generator to build out the container, one of those big, cumbersome, loud generators used on job sites that can power a welder. As the Houston hot and humid summer months drew near, and we needed to run the A/C in the container more often, we

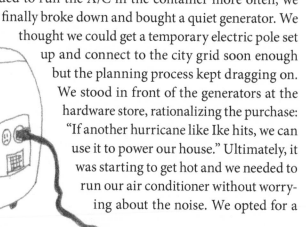

finally broke down and bought a quiet generator. We thought we could get a temporary electric pole set up and connect to the city grid soon enough but the planning process kept dragging on. We stood in front of the generators at the hardware store, rationalizing the purchase: "If another hurricane like Ike hits, we can use it to power our house." Ultimately, it was starting to get hot and we needed to run our air conditioner without worrying about the noise. We opted for a smaller, quieter Honda generator—a $1,000 investment. The generator can hold about one to one-and-a-half gallons of gas, which lasts about eight to ten hours. It primarily powered the A/C window unit, which routinely turned off in the early morning hours since the generator ran out of fuel after being on all night. At approximately $2.50 per gallon, we spent about $75 to $120 per month to run the generator, depending on how long and often we used it.

We also put a solar panel on the roof that charged a 12-volt battery with a 200-watt inverter, producing enough juice to power an indoor LED light or charge a phone or small fan. The solar panel was still active when we weren't home (we could keep a light or a fan on) but we did not keep the generator running. When we left for work in the morning, we opened the big doors of the container and the dogs were charged to patrol the property. Most likely, they just chased squirrels and sunbathed.

When we were home, we took full advantage of our unlimited data cell phone plan which is how we were able to access the internet. Cell phone reception and internet connection is pretty spotty inside of a metal box, so we found areas by the windows with the best reception. Most of the time, we streamed shows on our small cell phone screens. Using headphones, we could each binge watch shows separately; the world inside the container suddenly seeming much larger. I got through the cold winter months by eating soup and watching *Friday Night Lights*, Coach Taylor commanding "clear eyes, full heart, can't lose" as we slugged through the final stages of our planning process.

Not having continuous electricity also meant we couldn't keep a refrigerator and had to use coolers instead. We started with two coolers, maintaining our normal grocery shopping habits, but soon realized we had to shift to buying less fresh food and buying more packaged, canned, and dry goods. Even though we had to buy in smaller quantities—for example, a loaf of sliced bread was already too much—our food expenses increased. To buy healthy food in smaller packages costs more. We shifted to just one cooler: yogurt, milk, and eggs submerged in melted ice at the bottom and a system of larger plastic Tupperware floating at the top, keeping things dry and cool. We could have gone out to eat more or had things delivered but we didn't. The whole reason for living this way was to save money to build the house, and so we did.

Living off the grid made us acutely aware of all our resources and their limits. We realized how much gas (not just the cost but also the physical weight of the amount) we consumed to produce electricity. For example, lifting a gas can filled with three gallons of gas, trying to tilt it just right and hold it steady while pouring it into the small opening of the generator tank. Usually, we did this in the dark, either as the sun was coming up or going down, with a flashlight, making sure not to spill anything and guessing when it was full.

Dealing with a heavy gas can and jumpstarting the generator by pulling a cord was challenging. Thankfully Zak usually took care of this, although I vividly remember coming home one time while he was out and having to start the generator myself. I probably could have waited but it ended up becoming a point of pride: How hard could this be? It was raining. I marched from my car through the mud in my rain boots, sinking in here and there. The generator was under a wooden box, to keep it out of the rain and reduce the noise. I flipped the heavy box over, carried the generator (which was also heavy) into the bathhouse. I turned on the flashlight on my cell phone and positioned it on a table pointing at the ceiling to give me some ambient light. After positioning the funnel, I lifted the gas can (thankfully, it only had a gallon or so left so it wasn't too heavy) and steadily started pouring in the gas. After replacing the gas cap, I tried to start the generator. Full disclosure: I had never even started a lawnmower or anything that starts by pulling a cord. So, I went to town yanking and pulling, trying different strategies—fast, slow, fast; fast then slow— the generator slowly sputtering, teasing me into thinking something was happening. It was still raining outside, I was wet and now sweaty and sticky, and just wanted to turn on the damn A/C and relax. After what seemed like forever, the engine finally turned over, steadily purring away. I was exhausted but elated that I had done it.

Water

Similarly to electricity, we also had a container system for water. We filled five-gallon bottles with water at the various drinking water stations around town. Since we didn't have a bottle stand, we poured the water into a blue seven-gallon water jug with an "easy flow" spigot. From this we could easily (hence the easy flow) fill a one-gallon jug to keep inside to brush our teeth, wash dishes, cook, or fill our kettle to boil water. The blue easy flow jug also assisted in filling our five-gallon pressurized portable shower. We would boil one half-gallon of water and mix that with two to three gallons of cold water to have a warm shower. When the flexible water tank was filled and sealed, we stood it upright and used a foot pump to move air pressure into the tank. With enough pressure, we could then spray water out of an attached trigger-activated nozzle. The trick was to keep the pressure up as we used the water to wash. Also, it worked best in a crouching or seated position (despite the advertisements that show people standing while hosing themselves off after surfing all day) since the water didn't have to get pumped quite as high. Each shower was a different experience. Sometimes it was colder or hotter than expected, and we might actually get all the soap washed off without having to refill; sometimes the rhythm of spraying, pumping, and washing was beautifully orchestrated to give us a simultaneous leg workout. We did have a bathtub (a plastic animal trough) in the bathhouse. We discovered we could sit as if in a bathtub, place the pressurized tank between our legs, and position the pump against the side walls of the tub for easy pumping. We tried to recycle most of the water back into rain barrels to water plants, especially after taking showers or washing our hands. Despite having to physically haul water onto our property, we still maintained the yard.

To wash dishes, we soaped then stacked them in the sink, rinsed with cold water, closed the drain, poured boiling hot water over them, and covered with a dish towel to trap the steam. On average, we used approximately seven to ten gallons of water a day. We drove to fill up our five-gallon bottles every three or four days. Each cost $2, approximately $50 to $80 per month, depending on our usage. At the water fill stations, we also bought bags of ice to refill our coolers and keep our perishables cold. A twenty-pound bag costs around $1.75 and we bought one once a week, depending on how hot it was, for $8 to $10 per month.

Sewer

At first our sink drainage system was comprised of a bucket placed under the sink drain. When we drained pasta, we poured boiling water down into the drain and would have to pull out a steaming bucket of dirty water, open the container door, and empty it outside. We quickly upgraded by installing a pipe that took the water outside through the container floor.

This was our first and only plumbing upgrade. For most of our time living in the container, we used a composting toilet system. We took extra caution researching various methods and decided on a simple one that uses pine chips to keep things dry and odors neutralized. We used two buckets: a five-gallon orange bucket that said "Let's Do This" with a bucket-fitted toilet seat with lid (available at any camping store for about $6) and a small galvanized trash can that held the pine chips. The "Let's Do This" bucket had a layer of pine chips on the bottom and, after using the toilet, we scooped some more pine chips on top. Once the bucket was full, we had to dump it out. We sectioned off a small area in the back of the property and dug a hole to put our waste. We regularly covered the area with a thick layer of dirt to speed up the decomposition process; eventually, we dug another hole and the process started all over. Why go through all this and not just pay for a portable outhouse? Privacy. In addition to paying $130 per month in rental fees (which can add up quickly), it also has to be positioned along the driveway to provide easy access for the clean out trucks. Since we were near the back of the property, it would have been quite the trek every time we had to use the bathroom. Not a big deal except when it's late at night and we had to make our way through the darkness in our pajamas, not to mention if it's raining. Instead, pine chips cost approximately $5 per month and were easily purchased at a local feed store.

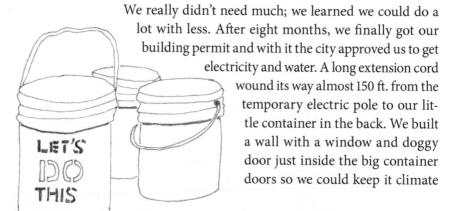

We really didn't need much; we learned we could do a lot with less. After eight months, we finally got our building permit and with it the city approved us to get electricity and water. A long extension cord wound its way almost 150 ft. from the temporary electric pole to our little container in the back. We built a wall with a window and doggy door just inside the big container doors so we could keep it climate controlled. We were able to finally plug in a mini-fridge and continuously use our A/C. No more getting up late at night to refill the generator or coming home late, in the rain, and trying to fill and start a generator in the dark. Or wanting to make a sandwich only to find that the deli meat bag was not closed all the way and the water from the melted ice in the cooler had soaked in despite all your efforts to keep things out of the water.

We didn't hook up the more than 200 ft. of hose to get water all the way to the bathhouse from the newly installed spigot by our ditch next to the street. We were happy to not have to drive to get water anymore. Now, we could just walk up to the front and fill up our one-gallon jugs whenever we wanted.

Memories

There were many memorable moments during our two-and-a-half years living in the container. Here are a few stories, in no particular order, from our adventures:

The time baby birds hatched

Our bath house had a decorative glass shelf where we kept garden supplies and tools as well as candles, mosquito spray, and a seemingly never-ending supply of koozies. The shelf was roughly 6 ft. high and, since it was outside, not the cleanest. Zak had a sturdy, plastic koozie with a leather, sculpted exterior complete with handle that he kept on the top shelf, a lucky gas station find. Through the winter months, the koozie kept getting pushed further back on the shelf, slowly slipping out of sight as new things got piled up in front. As the weather started to shift, it seemed that the top shelf was getting dirtier. For some reason, leaves and twigs were getting trapped. When I finally started the cleaning process, I thought it was odd that the koozie had leaves stuffed inside it. When I started to remove the debris, I realized a bird had made the koozie to a nest! Three small eggs were nestled in the cup. Surprised, happy, and startled, I replaced the leaves and returned the cup into its hiding place. I told Zak and we kept a close eye on the cup.

Weeks later as I went to use the bathroom, I heard a shrieking. I pulled away some of the things near the front of the shelf and saw all three baby birds—yellow beaks agape, eyes closed—had hatched and were hungry. I carefully put the cup back. When I went back later that day, the birds were still shrieking; later that night, same thing. Had mama bird forgotten about them? I started to worry we'd have to start collecting worms and take care of them, Googling "care for baby birds" but not really knowing what kind of birds they were. Thankfully mama bird hadn't forgotten them. They sure kept her busy—she was usually feeding them early in the morning and then went looking for more food. We kept the koozie where it was. Sometimes we'd hear them chirping, other times the rustling sounds made us aware they were still there. One morning, the sounds stopped. The birds were gone and we were finally able to clean out the koozie.

The time Zak roped a horse

Acres Homes is home to many animals—stray dogs, birds, Mexican eagles, wild parrots, and horses. The horses are kept almost like pets in the backyard or tied up in the front yard. Sometimes, the horses take themselves for a walk. One afternoon, a man stopped by and asked if we had seen two horses running through the neighborhood (he was missing two). Nope, but we would let him know if we did and we exchanged phone numbers. That evening was quiet with a full moon and a cool breeze blowing through. Suddenly, we heard horses galloping full speed down the street behind us. We realized those must be the missing horses and started yelling and clapping, hoping to draw their attention and sure enough we did. They turned on our street and, in the moonlight, majestically sped through our front yard, heading toward the fenced-in horses down the street.

Since they seemed to be distracted for awhile, we grabbed some rope and headed toward the horses. Zak managed to catch one but the other one took off. We kept our catch tied to a tree in our front yard overnight and for half of the following day until the owner stopped by to get her, thankful for our efforts. The other horse had found its way home safely.

The time we had donkeys

After living on Paradise for five months, we felt (somewhat) part of the neighborhood. Throughout the months, we talked to people who lived up and down the street, becoming friends with some of them and keeping an open mind when interacting with anyone in the neighborhood. But it seems we maybe overdid it in one situation.

One of the neighbors had acquired a mule. Not sure if he knew it at the time but she was pregnant. When she had her baby (the cutest, fluffiest donkey, ever), he kept them both tied to a tree in an empty lot just down the street. When he told us the owner of the lot had sold the land and he needed to find a new (and better) place to keep the donkeys, we generously offered to board them on our lot for a while until he found another location.

Almost two months later, he still hadn't found a place for the donkeys. Upon telling him that he really needed to contribute to the care of his animals if his search was taking this long, he handed us $10, only to later ask if he could borrow $50. Then he disappeared. Before leaving town for another month though, he bought us our very own donkey stallion as a "thank you" for boarding his animals. We named him Conkey.

Dealing with donkeys was pretty interesting; they are great animals, almost like dogs. They are very friendly and get attached pretty quickly, greeting us as we pulled up the driveway. The wooly baby donkey, Baby, grew up quickly and loved running around and playing with the dogs. She even started to roll over so we could rub her belly like a dog. But three donkeys, in addition to our two dogs, were a lot to take care of, especially considering we didn't have running water or electricity. And even though they make great lawnmowers, they don't distinguish between weeds and flowers—they eat everything. We built a little corral for them but keeping up with getting hay, cleaning stalls, and exercising them all became too much. And except for Conkey, they weren't really our donkeys.

It had become a sticky situation and quite unpleasant. After a few more months, lots of heartache, and much back and forth, we decided the donkeys needed to leave. I posted pictures of them on Facebook hoping that through social media's magic we could find them a proper home. Friends of mine shared the story and re-posted the picture on their pages and, through a strange coincidence, we found a match. A friend of a friend's parents were retired ranchers living on 700 acres in Blessing, Texas. They would love to take the donkeys.

I found an equestrian transport company to take them safely to Blessing, approximately 80 miles southwest of Houston. We waited anxiously in the front yard with the donkeys the morning of the pick up. Armed with carrots and apples, Zak, Jim, and I watched for the trailer. Finally, a monster of a vehicle resembling an exclusive RV pulled up in our small street. We immediately hit it off with the husband and wife team who ran the company and handled all transports. They were touched by our story and realized the special place these animals had carved out in our hearts. Mama Jenny and Baby waltzed right into their new, roomy quarters. Conkey was a bit hesitant but soon strutted in next to them. Once the trailer was locked up, we got into our cars and headed south.

Two hours later we turned off the highway onto a dirt road that led us to the ranch. Green fields lined both sides of the road with cows sporadically clustered throughout. We crossed paths with the new owners on the way. He was reserved, looked weathered, and sported a stiff plaid shirt with cowboy hat. She seemed to be the social one, rosy-cheeked with a floppy sun hat. Since it was still quite a distance to the ranch, the wife, in true old Texas fashion, without further discussion hopped out of their car and into ours, respectfully commandeering the situation, and giving directions as needed while chatting with us like we were old friends.

The ranch was beautiful. Live oak trees stretched their branches wide, almost leaning in for a side bend. We could see the fenced-in corrals of different sizes, each with a huge water tank. The house was in a typical ranch-style, a sprawling one-story rustic cabin with extended porch. Zak and I almost asked if we could be adopted as well.

The trailer with the donkeys pulled up to the smaller corral. The rancher opened the wide metal gate, leaning on it just so with one hand easily resting in his pocket. When the doors of the trailer opened, Mama Jenny stuck her head out, ears pointing straight up, and we could see her excitement build as she looked around. Mama Jenny was followed by Baby, and Conkey came out of the trailer last. They pranced into their new surroundings, ready to play with grandkids, protect cows, and just be.

The people of Blessing had originally applied to the federal government to name their city "God Bless, Texas." I'm sure the donkeys muttered an "Amen" as the sun set over their new home, filled with lush fields under the wide open Texas sky.

The time we had a cockroach in the container

The cockroaches usually came out at night, crawling along the floor, their flat, elongated, brown bodies looking like a walking cancerous mole, with antennas excitedly swishing back and forth as they explored their surroundings. Not frightening perse, but unexpected and unwelcome. They seemed unusually large, the palm of your hand providing a snug fit. The tiny hairs on their legs could be seen against the white color of the wall. I'm convinced it was the cramped quarters of our container that enhanced their size—within our small space they seemed huge.

Nighttime was the right time for them to make themselves known, usually right after Zak went to sleep and I was still awake. They knew who they were dealing with. The small space and lack of ventilation ruled out any roach spray. The best thing to do was to just swat them with a shoe or, as Zak liked to do, catch them with his bare hands and throw them back outside. But our tight quarters also meant less open floor space and many more hiding spaces, specifically under the bed. Our dogs, sadly, were of no use. They were interested enough to perk up but not motivated enough to actually move and kill.

Of course Zak was my preferred method of pest control and me not being the one to deal with it. I'm the kind of person who squishes a roach then leaves the shoe over the guts until someone else can clean it up. Or, until I am in a more mentally-prepared state to face it, using a set of long handled tools to scrape up the remains. I always make sure to wear closed-toe shoes during the hunt just in case the thing starts to play defense, charging my feet.

In short, I normally let others take the lead. Except when that person was sleeping, I had no choice. It usually worked like this: I would see something move out of the corner of my eye, realize what it was, and quietly start to stand up on a chair. I would start to call out Zak's name, getting louder every time the roach moved. By the time Zak would be awake and annoyed, it was out of sight. I would point and huff and puff, but he couldn't see anything. So he went back to sleep. After some time of it not reappearing, I would think it was safe and get ready for bed. Just before turning off the light, I would see it again (or was it a different one?) and this time it runs under the bed. And then I couldn't go to sleep. I would gently roll Zak over to the other side of the bed and flip up half of the futon to have access underneath. I saw it—it was in the perfect spot to be killed. I zeroed in, heart pumping, shoe in hand, and as I struck, pounding the ground multiple times, loud expletives escaped in between shrieks as I imagined the roach attacking me.

Then it was over. I won. And poor Zak let out a groan hoping for a quiet rest of the night.

The time we tried a DIY heating system

It was our first winter on the property and we still didn't have continuous electricity. Temperatures were starting to drop and we thought there had to be a better way than powering a space heater intermittently. It was such a small space. Just cooking on our camper stove put out enough heat to warm the container for a few hours. So we searched online and found some interesting blogs and videos of various options. We finally landed on a system of tea lights and clay pots since we already had the materials.

Start with a baking dish or tile, something that can handle very high heat without exploding. We used a bread pan and placed four tea lights at the bottom and placed a small clay plant pot (the kind with a drainage hole in the bottom) upside down over the tea lights, with the rim of the clay pot sitting on top of the bread pan. It is important that the tea lights still get plenty of air movement since otherwise the flame will go out. With the clay pot sitting upside down on the baking dish, we covered the pot's water draining hole at the top with a piece of aluminum foil. This is to ensure that the heat generated by the tea lights stays inside the pot and doesn't escape out of the top. Then we placed a slightly larger pot upside down so it completely covered the first pot but was still sitting on top of the bread pan. The smaller pot started to heat up from the tea lights underneath it. That

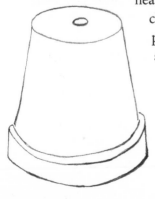

heat, since it has nowhere to go with the drainage hole closed up, radiates outward and, guided by the second pot, escapes through the top of the second pot. The second pot also helps with not getting burned, since that first pot gets pretty hot to the touch. Once the candles go out, the clay continues to radiate the heat.

We cuddled up on our futon couch, the clay pot contraption sitting just below us on the floor, and watched a movie.

The time we joined a gym

Zak and I are not "gym people." I typically feel like a hamster when running on a treadmill. All of those stationary activities with televisions seem kind of suspect to me. If I'm exerting energy, I want to be going somewhere. I don't want to pay to walk on a machine when I could walk outside in the park for free. I'd rather breathe in fresh air instead of recycled sweat.

Alas, the fall season, with its cooler temperatures, did finally arrive after a hot and humid summer in the container. We could open the windows again and use the generator less often but, since showering outside on a cool morning was not pleasant, we got a gym membership just to take showers. The gym also had a pool and sauna which was a definite plus with the approaching cold weather. And I did join with an open mind, giving this treadmill business another shot.

At first, I made sure it didn't look too obvious that I had rolled out of bed and was coming just to take a shower. I changed out of my pajamas into workout clothes, put on my tennis shoes, and pretended to head to a workout after putting my belongings in a locker. The front desk greeter was very impressed. After a month of checking me in every morning, he shot me a winning smile and said something like "Wow, you are doing great! You're here every day. Keep it up!"

A little embarrassed to be caught in a lie, I decided to quit pretending and just take a few minutes to exercise. The machines still didn't do it for me. I didn't like touching things on which other people's sweat had dripped all over, especially since many times they did not clean it up. But the pool ended up being worth my time and effort. I started swimming in the morning followed by five minutes in the sauna.

Although traditionally a relaxing, quiet, decompressing, and detoxing activity, the sauna was pretty weird. I think it is mainly used as a pre-workout "warm-up," a way to get sweating without doing anything. I would sit there in my bathing suit while other women crowded in wearing their nylon spandex workout gear with their headphones pumping music into their sweaty ears, filling the sauna with muffled beats. Other times, a woman would come in wearing what looked like a trash bag suit, presumably to accelerate and contain the sweat in hopes to lose more weight. The locker room ended up being a backdrop for selfies. Women got dolled up to pose in the mirror with the perfect hair-do before walking around the gym. It turned out I wasn't the only one pretending.

The time it flooded

Houston experienced serious flooding in the two-and-a-half years we lived in the container, the Memorial Day flood in May 2015 and the Tax Day flood in April 2016. Both times the water stopped just short of our threshold.

The first time in 2015, we just hunkered down. Thankfully, we were able to use our cell phones to find the live-stream of a local news station so we could watch as the hysteria unfolded. I know many people who went out that evening and got stuck or had their cars damaged. The last time Houston had a major flooding event was Tropical Storm Allison in 2001, so not too many people were worried. I think my moment of panic came when I opened the door to go out to our bath house and saw the water had already submerged the bottom step of our container. I watched as some of our garden supplies floated by. Armed with my umbrella and rain boots, I tried to make it to the bath house, sloshing through the calf-deep water, only to find everything bobbing off-kilter, the bricks completely covered with water. There was nothing we could do.

We stayed plugged into the live-stream on Zak's phone, using mine to check the radar and make phone calls, hoping the rain would just stop. The good thing was our building permit was approved at the beginning of the year so we were tied into the grid and didn't have to worry about the generator drowning. We also had a mini-fridge so we could eat and cook without having to go outside. But, in case the power did go out, we were fully prepared. We just watched and waited.

The next time I opened the door, the water was only a few inches below the threshold. We started to move items away from the door and tried to get valuables off the floor in case water came in. Thankfully, it finally stopped in the early morning hours and we could get some sleep. That morning when I opened the door, I could only see a lake that spanned multiple properties. The water was almost as deep as our rain boots were high but we made it. And it made us aware of the low spots of our property, how the flood waters recede, and what we needed to watch out for.

The Memorial Day flood dropped 162 billion gallons of water on Houston. Eleven months later the Tax Day Flood brought 240 billion gallons of water in roughly the same time frame of a just a few days.[29] Despite the steep increase, the good news was that our experience didn't really change much from the Memorial Day flood, even though we had our foundation piers drilled, subfloor installed, and some exterior walls framed. As part of the site preparation, we also had our civil engineering in place—a shallow mote that made its way around the house and carried the water to the front ditch. The water still rose just as high as before around our container and house but because we had built at the correct height, everything worked as it should.

Many other people were not so lucky. As we hunkered down—again glued to the live-stream of the news on our phone—we saw for the first time parents pushing their kids to safety in refrigerators through the flood waters as they themselves were waist deep in water. Boats were dispatched to neighborhoods, animals and owners were pulled out of chest-high flooded houses and apartment buildings. People in big trucks with raised cabs, often ridiculed by outsiders as the quintessential Texas tough symbol, became heroes as they barreled across the city, making multiple trips into neighborhoods, rescuing as many people as they could. Say what you want about those freedom-loving Texans but when shit hits the fan—or billions of gallons of water are dropped on the city—they are quick to respond and lend a helping hand.

Once the rain stopped, we walked around our construction site, taking note of any damage. We were really lucky.

The time Zak made an art car

Around the time we bought our property, Zak made the decision to go back to school. As he was finishing up his associate's degree, he happened to help deliver a sculpture to a local university. The art faculty courted him, showed him the facilities, and he ended up enrolling for his undergraduate degree in art. Through research and orientation he learned the school, as a private, faith-focused university, had an additional requirement for graduation: acquiring "community life and worship points." These can usually be satisfied through various on-campus worship activities like Bible study but students could also petition for outside activities. As we had just moved into Acres Homes with an elementary school just down the street, he wanted to create some kind of partnership between the two schools to make an art car for the next parade. As a son of the Urban Animals, Zak had essentially grown up with art cars, which are vehicles transformed by artists into sculptures on wheels that are then rolled out in an annual parade through downtown Houston.

Zak reached out to Rebecca Bass, an educator and former Urban Animal who spearheaded the use of art car projects in educational settings as tools to teach life skills and engage students with their schools and communities, to help with his vision for our community project. She helped make introductions and advocated for the project as a good experience for the students. Along with a few university students, Zak would construct the elements which the fifth graders would paint. Students from the university would visit the elementary school once a week for a one-hour afterschool program to paint and decorate but also teach about art, drawing, and making 3-D objects. The elementary school principal was on board and excited to offer this to their students; the faculty at the university were thrilled as well to be involved in a cross-pollination project. The Art Car Partnership was formed.

The project needed funds for a car and supplies and it just so happened that United Airlines was looking for a community-based art car project to sponsor as part of their outreach programs. They had just launched their non-stop flights to Santiago, Chile, and wanted the project to incorporate the destination in some way with a budget of $5,000. Zak revamped the project to feature the Mercado Central Market, which is one of the top destinations in Santiago, and submitted his idea to United. His proposal was accepted. He acquired a car, built a structure on it that was architecturally inspired by the market, and the hood of the car became a colorful fruit stand.

The crossover between the two schools presented a brilliant educational exchange. Not only were the students learning about another country and another culture, but also about a future in the arts, what it means to be an artist, and the possibilities of higher education. The grant also provided funds for a shuttle and snacks to make sure the kids were able to attend the parade downtown. Most of them had never been to or seen anything like it. The parade in recent years has grown to attract more than 250 vehicles from twenty-three states. The streets were lined solid with 250,000 or more spectators. And, in the midst of all this, was their art car.

The time Zak proposed

When I decided to go to school in Los Angeles, I never thought I would move back to Houston. But when I left for California, my car crammed full of stuff, headed west on I-10, I felt so conflicted. I had just met Zak and, before we could figure out where our interest in each other would lead, I had to leave and he was sent to the Persian Gulf for a three month assignment through the Seafarers International Union, shuttling between Dubai, Qatar, and Bahrain. Our communication, which had been almost daily, dropped down to sporadic phone calls when he had a signal. I could send emails to a general inbox, which were then printed out (probably scanned for threats), and slipped under his door. We would see each other when I was home during the holidays.

My first semester of school was somewhat of a shock and I considered leaving. I had progressed steadily as an artist in Houston but that didn't matter much in graduate school. The faculty and my peers wanted to know why they should care about my artwork and I didn't yet understand why making an argument for my art was important. One day, I crossed paths with one of my professors and told him I was thinking about quitting the program. He encouraged me to stay, saying that there might be a reason for me to be here, at this point in my life, with these people, to have this experience. I always think about that hallway pep talk whenever I feel stagnant. Somehow, there is a reason why I'm here at this moment.

I decided to stay and those two years might be the reason why I'm writing this book. But I grew to really miss Houston—the community, the weirdness of the city, the people. Zak and my mom were a big pull and, by the time I started my second year of school, there was no question about me moving back. During my winter break, Zak and I looked for places to rent and found our little bungalow. We signed the lease a few days before I headed back to school.

Taking the dive and making major life decisions seemed to be our thing, so it's no surprise that two months after we moved into the container, he proposed. As usual, he woke up early, refilling the generator to keep the air conditioning going while I continued sleeping. He made coffee and, as the scent filled the container, woke me up and proposed. There I was—in my pajamas, unwashed with morning breath and engaged. I couldn't believe it; it had been a complete surprise. Zak opened a window and yelled across the yard to Jim and the rest of the neighborhood: "She said YES!" Beaming, I finally climbed out of bed, stepped outside of the container and made my way to the composting toilet wearing my new engagement ring.

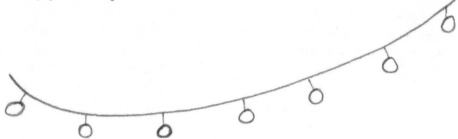

The time we had people over

We really like hosting parties, dinners, and similar. When we lived in our little bungalow, we started an Easter brunch tradition. We made Bloody Marys and a grilled feast for our friends and family with fresh homemade salads to complement. Living in a container put a damper on those kinds of plans since most guests like having access to a flushing toilet and air conditioning.

But that didn't stop us from still inviting people. We cleaned the bathroom before our guests arrived, placed some flowers in a vase, put out a fresh hand towel with the hand soap, and explained to everyone how to use the composting toilet; though intrigued, no one really took us up on it. I served drinks, wet, out of our coolers and we would sit outside under the trees. People grew steadily more and more uncomfortable. I watched as the sweat beads piled up on their foreheads and their breathing quickened. They would start getting flushed, usually making a quick exit after one or two drinks. Therefore, having an engagement party on our property was a bit awkward. But when I came home from work that evening, I saw my soon-to-be mother-in-law washing vegetables in our little container sink, using the makeshift water pump and getting things ready for the grill. We plugged in a large outdoor fan, along with some lights, and set a big, round table with lots of chairs. We bought mosquito spray in bulk. We served food inside our container on the countertop, salads on our little dining table. We turned the A/C on so people could have some refuge from the heat when they prepared their plates of food. People stayed as long as they could and we actually had some takers for the composting toilet.

People always ask me if I would do it all over again if I had to and I always say yes. It was a unique learning experience. Those two-and-a-half years taught me a lot about myself, self-sufficiency, and stretching my limits. The experience made me grateful for all the comforts we enjoy on a regular basis. The most wonderful thing, right next to the invention of the modern sewer system, is to have hot water on demand. It still blows my mind that we can turn on a faucet and have hot water whenever we want—it is truly the most luxurious thing we have.

In general, this process has taught me a lot about people—what motivates them, the systems in which they operate, and how little room there is for difference. Everyone follows a set pattern and if we fall outside of that it is hard to get ahead. There are rules, guidelines, we are supposed to follow.

But falling outside of those neatly drawn lines also means freedom, freedom to be in control of our own lives. This is why I think movements such as tiny houses and "van life" have become such a phenomenon—people feel that they are regaining control. 2018 saw an increase of 17 percent in travel trailers since 2017.[30] We might not be able to control the world at large but within our van, tiny house, box, or trailer, each of us is the person in charge to make decisions that directly impact our lives. Ultimately, it is also a creative pursuit; everyday presents a unique challenge. For example, how could you recreate a faucet without plumbing and running water? The constant problem-solving keeps the mind nimble and body aware. a house with a mortgage, utilities, and building codes is very much tied into an existing approved system, those neatly drawn lines.

CHAPTER SEVEN

Planning

We took a big leap of faith by moving into the container. We were counting on getting utilities set up as soon as possible but we learned that we first needed a building permit. To apply for a residential building permit, we needed to collect a variety of data, forms, and documents. The best thing to do is to check with the local permit office—either look through their resources online or visit their offices and talk to someone. It can seem like a long and scary process but whether you are dealing with permit officers or inspectors, they are just people doing a job and they want to help.

This is a list of required items that we filed for a residential single-family building permit in the City of Houston:[31]

- **Building Permit Application:** A simple form available online explaining what we were planning to build, square footage, estimated cost of improvement to the property, our contact info, and the contact info of our contractor. This generated a project number that became the account number to look up the progress of our submitted plans, notes of corrections, etc.
- **Plat Plan:** We purchased this at the City of Houston permit office to show how the lots in the neighborhood are platted.
- **Geographic Information and Management Map:** From the city website, we downloaded the GIMS map outlining the city infrastructure of our immediate neighborhood.
- **Soil Test:** We hired a local soil testing company (also known as geotechnical engineer) to examine a soil sample from our property to determine how deep the foundation had to be.
- **Elevation Certificate:** We hired a certified surveying company to determine how high our property is above sea level which indicated the minimum height for our finished floor based on our area's current floodplain data.

- **Plans (two sets):** The kind of house you want to build, for example prefabricated versus a custom design, determines if you need to hire an architect. Even though we had our own hand-drawn designs, we still needed someone to digitally render our plans. The architect was also familiar with the building codes, and was able not just to render floor plans but also a site plan, side elevations, and electrical plans.
  - **Floor Plans:** Architectural plans delineating room layout, width of walls, size of windows, gas line stubs, etc.
  - **Site Plan:** A bird's eye view of the property, noting any trees that will exist (part of the landscaping requirement), where the house will be located in relationship to the fence line, where the driveway will be, and what materials will be used.
  - **Electrical:** Once the floor plans are in place, the architect or designer will also generate an electrical plan that shows where lights and fans will be installed, where the light switches will be located, as well as A/C and other mechanicals.
  - **Side Elevations:** All four side views of the house, showing the exterior with window and door placement. They will also generate a cross section that shows the interior.
- **Structural and Civil Engineering Plan (two sets):** The architect will send the licensed engineer the generated floor plans and the engineer will generate the structural and civil drawings. Structural drawings detail the framing plan, roof structure, foundation, etc. Civil plans are like a mash-up of the site-plan and the elevation certificate, adding in grading of the land to help water flow away from the house.
- **Energy Code Docs:** We submitted a REScheck, which looks at plans and takes into consideration the type of wall insulation, type of windows, and number of doors and generates an energy rating. Once the house is complete, there is something called the "blower door test" that needs to be done by the same company, ensuring that the pressure is as initially indicated.
- **Excavation and Fill Worksheet:** We downloaded this from the city permit office website. It is a worksheet that determined if we needed a special grading permit based on the amount of dirt mechanically added or removed from the site.
- **Wastewater Capacity Reservation Letter:** We first had to submit the wastewater capacity reservation application to the city informing them of what we planned to build. They sent us back the WCR letter with an

assessment of the fees (impact fees) we had to be pay. When we submitted the plans, the application, receipt of impact fee payment, and letter from the city had to be included.

- **Analysis of Impervious Cover Worksheet:** A worksheet we downloaded from the city website to note square footage of our improvements that are impervious cover, for example piers and driveway.

- **Application for Sidewalk Variance:** Our site plan showed the driveway (note type of paving), sidewalks, and ditches and addressed right-of-way. An experienced architect will know what markers need to be included. We had to submit an application for sidewalk variance to verify that we didn't need to/couldn't add a sidewalk due to the ditches running alongside our side of the street.

- **Residential Landscape Analysis Form:** This is another worksheet we downloaded from the city website that asks questions about the trees located between the street and right of way (for us, the first 25 ft. from the street). Since we had the two required trees still in place, we had to note the size and type of tree. If we would have had none, then we would have had to plant two trees (the number of trees is based on the size of the lot).

- **Building Permit Fee:** We had to pay this at the end before receiving our permit; typically, the amount is determined by the valuation of the home.

No building permit application will be the same because no project is the same, and no city permit office or officer is the same. You won't really get into the thick of things until you start submitting your materials, talking to people, asking questions. But it is never too early to start. It will probably take approximately one year to even like your floor plans. The actual permitting process might take six to twelve months, depending on corrections and who or what you are waiting on. The building process could take twelve, eighteen, twenty-four months, or longer. Start early and don't get discouraged. It's going to be hard *and* fun.

Our plans:

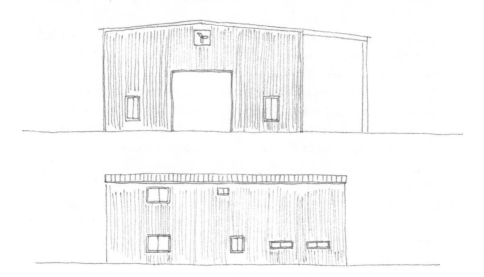

The home Zak and I envisioned before we even owned property was a 40 x 60 sq. ft. metal building on a concrete slab foundation. It was divided into two-thirds house and one-third workshop, oriented lengthwise with the shop section (including a big roll up door) and exhaust fan just below the roof peak facing the street. The 40 x 40 sq. ft. living section was an open floor plan with a stylish spiral staircase leading up to a loft area and master suite. A second bedroom, office area, and bathroom, along with kitchen, dining, and living room, were on the first floor. The bathrooms, utility room, and kitchen were all stacked to consolidate the plumbing into one area of the house. Both bathrooms had separate tubs and shower stalls, and the toilet was placed out of sight. The stairs wound their way up to the master suite and loft/library area. The master bath had standard double sinks. The kitchen was sizable but not too large with a big island complete with stove top and bar seating for three. The dining room table sat eight people and there were big sliding glass doors that opened to the back yard. The workshop was mainly open, with a third bathroom and small office as the only adjacent rooms. With all this space, open area to stretch, we still asked ourselves questions such as, "Is a 14 x 14 sq. ft. bathroom/utility room too small? Is a 10 x 14 sq. ft. bedroom adequate? Are two 10 ft. wall spaces enough for master suite closets?"

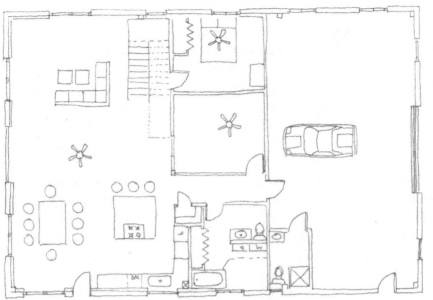

I'm still pretty proud of our first set of drawings. Without either of us having any architectural training, the flow of the rooms and the layout worked pretty well. Zak dictated mechanical efficiency and I looked for design and space efficiency. I made a scale model out of foam board so we could move around the walls, maybe even place a scaled couch, dining table, and kitchen island. It was like playing with a dollhouse. We landed on a configuration we liked and we needed someone with AutoCAD skills and some experience drawing plans to realize them.

My sister Diana had studied architecture at the University of Houston. Since she is eight years older than me, she was already well into her college studies while I was just starting high school. Maybe all those nights of her assembling tiny windows and beams in her bedroom, leaving in the morning with finished detailed scale models, influenced some of my desire to design my own. She moved back to Germany soon after graduating and, although she still worked with real estate, she hadn't used AutoCAD in years and wasn't familiar enough with the U.S. building code standards needed to draw the plans. She found a former classmate who still lived and worked in Houston who was interested in working with us. She was also a bit rusty—she worked more on the engineering side of planning subdivisions—but could help us. We emailed our drawings to her and in a couple of weeks she sent us a set of blueprints complete with floor plans, electrical plans, and elevations.

Having accomplished this first step, we met with a contractor. We had been courting Oscar for months. We asked people with industrial metal houses who had been their contractor and his name kept coming up, highly recommended. We learned that he was friends with people we knew through the arts and actually lived nearby. Though I'm sure he is solicited often, he was kind enough to meet with us over drinks to look at and discuss our plans. Since we would eventually need a lender-approved contractor for a construction loan, we thought he might be our guy.

In his calm and composed manner, he reviewed our plans, asked questions where needed, and became a voice of reason for us in this process. He informed us that we couldn't have a spiral staircase leading to the second floor if there is a bedroom upstairs since a spiral staircase as our only point of egress is a fire hazard; the workshop area should be labeled "two-car garage" so as to not be considered commercial; there needed to be a firewall between our garage and living space, complete with self-closing doors, and more. We made the changes. Instead of three bedrooms and an office, our plans showed two bedrooms and an office. The upstairs layout shifted sides. The downstairs bathroom also became the laundry room. Our mechanical closet moved on top of the shop/garage bathroom. In addition to technical feedback, Oscar was also the first person to make me realize how long planning and building a house could take. He mentioned that even though he had seen the process take a year, most likely it would be three years or more, much to my discontent. I still remember when he asked if we were good at making decisions, looking at us with a steady gaze, gauging just how committed we really were. We were getting ready to decide a whole lot.

Jim was in the same boat as we were. He had been hand-drawing his plans over coffee and beers, laying out the structure in detail, the rooms, what he needed, what he wanted. He was going for an octagon-shaped cabin, two stories with wrap-around porches. It was a sturdy building with substantial wind resistance and maximum space efficiency. He realized he knew someone who had a construction consulting firm. Noah mainly worked on structural and civil engineering plans for big commercial projects. Since he liked Jim and owed him a favor (because everyone owes Jim a favor), Noah said he was willing to help Jim get his building permit.

Zak and Jim met Noah at his office to go over Jim's plans. Noah said he could also take a look at our project and possibly be the engineer for it and to send him what we have. Upon sending him our plans, we were in for a huge surprise: we couldn't have a slab foundation. He detailed that due to the size of our lot and it being in a floodplain, our finished floor would have to be 1 ft. above the floodplain. Not only would that increase the amount of concrete we would need for the slab (more expensive) but it would create an enormous amount of impervious cover. The city would require a retention pond that would be almost the size of our slab.

His email explanation was yet another reality check for Zak and me. We purchased the land knowing it was in the floodplain but, beyond having to pay extra flood insurance, we didn't really know how that would impact our construction. We needed some guidance, not just concerning our floor plans but also what type of house we could build given the situation of the land. So, we decided to ask Noah what our options were.

A floodplain is an area of low-lying ground located near a river, or bayou in Houston's case, that is prone to flooding. The Houston area is just barely above sea level; some areas of downtown are only 40 ft. high. Harris County is divided into 100-year and 500-year prone flood areas. The Harris County Flood Education Map shows where each one is sited as well as where designated floodways (areas closest to the bayou in which structures are not allowed to be built) are located.

But as a Harris County Appraisal District advisor recently told me, the whole damn city is essentially a floodplain. Recent flood events, specifically Hurricane Harvey, created such unprecedented amounts of flooding and damage—even in areas that didn't previously flood—that it really questions the idea of maps and flood designation points for development. By the time the next storm hits, the maps will already be out of date and many more homes will be flooded. The culprit: impervious cover, also known as concrete. (Climate change and its array of causes are also factors but I'm thinking more on a local scale.) The more the city expands, the more green space—wetland, grassland —is being covered by concrete for development. As Houston keeps expanding, all of the development—infrastructure, housing—leaves little ground to soak up water. As a city that has been erected from a swamp, there is no escaping the water. The best option is to cooperate with it and give it some space.

The solution for our future flood-prone home site ended up being pier and beam, which is the way houses used to be built in the Houston area. Pier and beam foundation is exactly that—a configuration of vertical piers matched with horizontal beams to form an elevated platform on which a house is built. The piers are driven deep into the soil until they hit ground that is more stable than what is located near the surface. Land in Houston is very rich in clay which makes it fluctuate based on the weather conditions. When it's wet, it expands, and when it's dry, it contracts. Although elevated, this makes for a much stronger foundation than a slab foundation, which is concrete poured directly on a graded level ground. The elevation, or crawlspace, in addition to providing easy access for any plumbing or mechanical fixes, allows for water to flow and soak back into the ground. The crawlspace is also advantageous in this climate since it allows for air circulation, helping to naturally keep the house cool which saves on energy cost. Pier and beam foundation is much pricier than the now-popular slab foundation but it saves money in the long run. We hadn't really considered pier and beam for our new construction but it seemed like the better—and really only—choice we had. Sadly, this meant we had to reconfigure our house.

While Zak and Jim were at Noah's office, Noah introduced them to Jamie who was renting office space from him. Jamie was young, energetic, eager, and recognized an opportunity. We needed new plans and someone to guide us; Jamie knew AutoCAD, was new to construction, and trying to get his foot in the door. He presented us with some quickly sketched options for our house. We asked about cost for the construction, if a $100 per sq. ft. would be applicable. He said he could do it for $85 per sq. ft. Since I had just learned about debt to income calculations, I realized that I could qualify for a $130,000 loan, meaning the house could only be 1,300 sq. ft., a considerable drop from our expansive 2,400 sq. ft. warehouse.

Jamie took our basic open layout with loft and master suite upstairs and reconfigured it into a 25 x 30 sq. ft. house, yielding us a total living space of 1,200 sq. ft. Porches came off the front and back like little fins. I don't think

Jamie had much experience working with clients on the design process, so he got a bit overzealous and thought he could realize his dreams with our house. We now had two doors on the street-facing side: the front door and, essentially right next to it, a door into the utility room which now was also labeled "mudroom." When Zak and I sat down for a meeting to go over the plans, and I finally met Jamie in person, I realized that sprawling hip-roofs, designated mud rooms, large kitchens, and country style windows all represented "the good life" for Jamie, and he was going to make sure we had it. He wore a fancy watch, a standard polo shirt with khaki pants, and addressed Zak as "Bro," not only in person but also in all email communication. He explained that one of the advantages of having a separate entrance meant shoes caked with mud didn't spoil the clean house, and gave a wink in my direction. (Couldn't the shoes just be removed outside? Isn't that what porches are for?) As he reviewed plans for the kitchen area, he leaned closer to me to point out the layout for cooking appliances. I finally stopped him and said, "You're talking to the wrong person. Zak does most of the cooking." The downstairs shower and toilet had moved to the other side of the kitchen wall, another standard design element in most houses and one I can't stand.

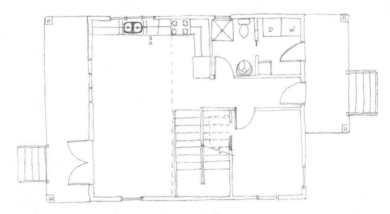

In addition to the two street-facing doors, it was the side elevations that stopped me in my tracks. Our clean, industrial-style design had taken the shape of a convoluted suburban house. It had a hip roof (in which all four corners go up at an angle to then create a saddle shape over the house), and the porches had separate roofs that jutted out front and back, with weird, ornate-looking columns holding them up, plus a tiny roof within the larger roof to house an attic exhaust. We had been so focused on the warehouse aesthetic, which is pretty standard, I hadn't even thought about what a non-industrial house would look like.

We were living in the carriage house at the time and, when I took the dogs on walks around the immediate neighborhood, I studied every house, thinking to myself, "Well, this one has the weird attached front porch. Could I live in something like that?" and, "They have that attic exhaust extension; I guess it doesn't look that bad." I became obsessed. Everywhere I went, I would stop and study houses. Where was the front door in relation to the porch? How did the railing look? What shape was the roof? Where were the windows? It was as if we were back at square one.

With our lack of financial resources to pay for additional edits to our plans (we had already paid almost $3,000), I felt pressured to continue with what we had, and not sweat a detail like roof formation (hip roofs are actually more durable when it comes to hurricanes). I also felt pressured to quit making adjustments and just say "O.K." because "O.K." meant we could move on to the next phase of submitting plans to get a building permit which would mean getting finally utilities set up on our land. Zak kept reminding me of our small bungalow which had been just fine for us. All we needed now was something just a little bit bigger.

But, honestly, if something doesn't feel right, it probably isn't, which is different than being scared to take a step. Reluctantly, I resolved to just go with it—this weird suburban house on stilts—so we could move on.

Then, oddly, Jamie started stalling. First, it was because the floodplain maps were being redrawn by the Federal Emergency Management Agency and we had to wait for the new ones to see if our situation had changed. Then, he was supposed to have print-outs of our plans, yet they were somehow always at the printer but never finished. He gave us the run around for six months. Zak would schedule a meeting and Jamie wouldn't show up, or he would call back hours later to say he got delayed and he'd be there within the hour but would never show. We had paid him 50 percent up front, approximately $2,000 in cash, before all this started happening. We thought he would want the remaining 50 percent and do a good job for us. We thought wrong.

Jim, who was in the same predicament as us with his plans, and I decided to pay Jamie an unexpected visit. We showed up bright and early to his office but no sign of him. Noah, who was patiently waiting with us, ended up hearing our story first hand. He called Jamie on speaker phone and, again, he was "just around the corner and would be in shortly," the same spiel we had been getting for months. Of course, he didn't show up. Noah called him back, frustrated, and at this point I was fuming. I took over the conversation and, interspersed with expletives, told him that we will not be continuing his service and wanted our money back. Realizing how important timing is in the building process, we decided to cut our losses and work with someone else. We never saw Jamie or our m~~

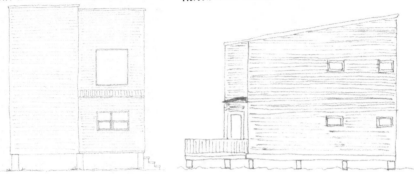

Diana's plans

During this flare up, my sister arrived for a short vacation. I had discussed with her our property and plans over many months but she had never seen either in person. When she finally did see them, she wasn't excited either. She validated my intuition that something didn't feel right—the whole thing just didn't fit. She didn't understand why we were doing a hip roof and not a shed roof (one-direction slanted roof). The answer we got from Jamie was that the hip roof is more common and, therefore, cheaper. She didn't believe it. A shed roof would require a lot less structure and a metal roof would be more durable than roofing tiles.

Aesthetically, she concurred that the exterior didn't fit the modern loft layout. It was also oriented squarely, which did not maximize the space in the most efficient manner. The open area was across the shorter end of the 25 x 30 ft. rectangle. As she rehashed all the things I instinctively knew to be wrong with the plans, I realized my worst fear was happening: Zak and I were stressed about building a house we didn't love, hoping other people wouldn't see it that way. But she saw it.

It is probably the worst thing for an architect to see a poorly designed house being built. Unbeknownst to me, my sister thought about our plans, priorities, size restrictions, land, trees, and more, and stayed up late to design the house we have today, drawn on 8.5 x 11 in. printer paper using a pencil, eraser, and her old architectural ruler she found at our mom's house during her visit. The result was two new sets of floor plans and exterior elevations.

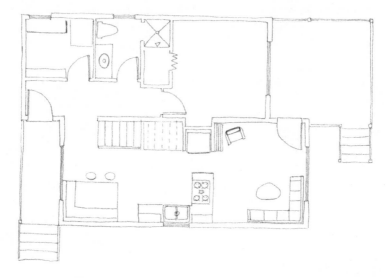

Her design split the 25 x 30 ft. house footprint in half and shifted it parallel 5 ft., creating space for the porches. The elongated rectangular shapes, roughly 13 x 30 ft, repeated the elongated rectangular shape of our lot, 65 x 330 ft. The living, kitchen, and dining areas were all in one half of the house, the loft was above the kitchen, with a 20 ft. tall area opening up on either side in the living and dining areas. The master suite was on the second floor, taking up a quarter of the house. Utility room, guest bath, and guest bedroom were underneath, separated from the common areas by the staircase.

Viewed from the front, the split house had a yin-yang feeling: the recessed side, giving way to the front porch, had large windows where the other half had none facing the street. All windows were directed towards the back-yard, providing privacy to the front. The shed roof sloped towards the back, giving the house an elongated towering presence. When viewed from the street, it seemed to be reaching towards the sky, just like the surrounding trees. It was perfect.

Before my sister went back to Germany, she met up with some friends from her architectural school days at UH. Since college, many of them had stayed in the field and, thankfully, one of them was willing and able to translate Diana's hand-drawn plans into AutoCAD blueprints. We had a new

set of professionally-drawn plans—floor plans, side
elevations, site plan, and electrical—in three weeks.

Jamie had also been in charge of our structural
and civil engineering plans but, because he burned
the bridge with the engineer, we never received the
finalized plans and needed replacement drawings.
Although self-drawn plans can be submitted to the
city, the structural and civil plans have to be stamped
by a licensed engineer. I contacted a company that
came highly recommended by an associate who
works in development. They required 40 percent of
the $4,500 total as a down payment before they got
started which made me a little squeamish. Thankfully, they stuck around for the remaining 60 percent, showed up for meetings and, in general, were
a pleasure to work with.

In the end, it was good to get a second opin-
ion. Our previous civil engineering plan included
a drainage ditch that wrapped around the whole
property at the border. The new engineers came
to do a site visit and, upon realizing we were not
making any changes to the back of the property,
simply marked it as "undeveloped land" on the plans.
The result was a drainage ditch that only wrapped
around our driveway and house, carrying the excess
water towards the street into the city ditches.

Now that we had our plans, we could make our
way through the building permit requirements.
We printed our plans at the official size of 30 x 40
in. and on November 3, 2014, we submitted our
first complete batch of paperwork to apply for the
building permit— almost a year-and-a-half after
we purchased the property and seven months after
moving in to the container.

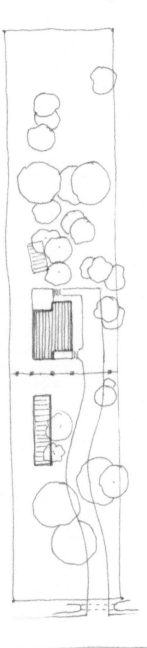

PARADISE LANE

Permit

As these things go, we were, of course, rejected and received a long list of corrections and details to be revised. Most of these corrections can be forwarded to the architect or engineer so they can make the adjustments. There were a couple of things none of us understood, especially the notes regarding the landscaping plan. Apparently, we had to keep two trees but anyone looking at our site plan could see that we kept more than twenty trees on our property. I decided to go to the permit office and, while submitting revisions, see if I could ask someone to clarify the landscaping issue.

Normally, a contractor or builder has permit runners as part of their team whose job it is to follow up on plans at the permit office, meet with people, file updated paperwork, and similar. Since Zak and I were the only people dealing with the permitting, we made it work and alternated. Now, it was my turn.

The permit building was actually pleasant to visit—new, modern, and aiming for maximum efficiency. It sported big displays about the benefits of green building and energy efficiency. I looked in the directory to find which floor I needed to be on and, once there, I signed in, took a number, and had a seat. The crowd was mixed, diverse, and about half of the people in the room looked like this was their job, indicated by the way they nodded at each other in acknowledgement and seemed to be familiar with the people behind the desks.

When my number was called, I followed a man not much older than me through a set of double doors into a big room filled with rows upon rows of cubicles. I had envisioned a dark, dusty carpeted maze but the space was lit by big windows in the old brick walls on all sides. People were bustling, talking with clients at their desk, wheeling around carts full of plans, phones were ringing, papers were shuffling. This was the belly of the building and permit office for the fourth largest city in the U.S. and it kind of reminded me of Willy Wonka's Chocolate Factory.

We made small talk, then sat down at his desk. I handed over my documents and we discussed the notes. It was a surprisingly personal process. He was part of the structural engineering department and seemed to be new on the job. We both tried to make sense of the changes that needed to be addressed and, after much discussion, he found a more experienced city employee a couple of cubicles over who was able to help us. Between the two of them, I was able to fully understand the problem and what needed to happen in order to satisfy city code and get our structural approval.

I then had to go and get another number and wait to talk to someone from the landscaping division regarding the trees. The man who retrieved me clarified that the two trees had to be within 25 ft. of the street, and we didn't have any trees marked on the site plan. We did actually have two smaller trees that qualified (the city has a list of approved trees) but somehow we had not included them on our site plan. He then wrote down his city email address so I could send him the updated site plan and he could approve it in the system instead of it landing on somebody else's desk. I asked about the approval process and why it takes so long to turn around plans. He just pointed to the exterior brick wall behind me which was lined with plans rolled in tubes of various sizes, stacked three deep. "We are doing the best we can but we are just swamped." Within two months, we were notified of approval and were ready to pay for our building permit.[32]

Approved

I still remember the day I paid for our building permit. I was sitting in the waiting area, plans in hand, waiting for my number to be called. I felt nervous, a little teary-eyed, and somewhat giddy. When it was finally my turn, the woman asked about the reason for my visit and I proudly stated, "My plans were approved!" No fanfare, no smile—just business as usual as she asked for my building permit number. She took my payment, I signed some papers, and then she handed me my yellow permit slip with the receipt stapled to it. "Well, here you go. All set." I took the piece of paper and looked at her. No folder or binder? She looked at me blankly, what kind of folder was I looking for? "Well, like, a folder outlining next steps, with all the necessary forms, phone numbers to call, when to call." Nope, that was it. I could find all the information online. So I left with my approved plans, $712.62 poorer and binder-less but a big step forward. We were ready to build.

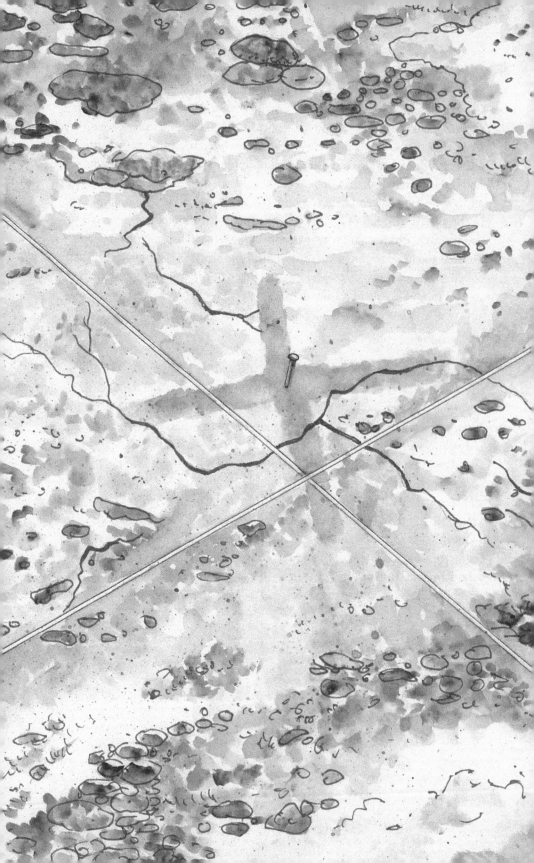

CHAPTER EIGHT

Financing

M ost people hate to discuss their finances. Just the mere mention can send people reeling, desperately searching for a way out of the discussion. The question "How are you making it all work?" could be just around the corner. The true financial picture is revealed: How are you funding your lifestyle? This is exactly what happens when purchasing or building a house. You will be examined, poked, prodded, and squeezed like a hog going up for auction. You're the pig and the lenders are the farmers getting you prepped for underwriting, deciding if you are even worth the trouble.

Personal finances

This house was going to be the biggest financial investment Zak and I had made. Pretty much anybody you talk to about building or buying a house will always have a personal financial hardship story, like eating only soups or beans and rice for years since that was all they could afford. There will be upfront costs to plan for as well as those unexpected surprises during the construction period. No need to sugarcoat it: The process can drain you financially if you are not careful.

When starting the process of getting your finances in the right place, it is also a good time to take a closer look at your personal budget and build in some savings. How much money are you spending on food? How often are you eating out? What is the total cost of your subscription services? Could you refinance your car loan? How about a lower car insurance payment? Do you really need that gym membership? How much money could you set aside to build your house? Create a reasonable budget for yourself and stick with it. The answer to most financial situations is usually not more money but spending less.[33]

Zak and I had approximately $10,000 in savings and $5,000 in our checking account when we started this process. Each bill had an impact but, since the project stretched over many years, we were diligent to always replenish our stash between purchases so we could be ready for that next big expense.

Ultimately, getting feedback will be an important part of this puzzle. Tell anyone and everyone who will listen what you are trying to accomplish—you never know who can help or has a friend of a friend who can assist. Many of the key players in making our dream a reality were just that: friends of friends, who happened to have time and wanted to help. As you move through this process, you'll be doing a lot of financial assessments, but don't forget to take stock of your social capital as well.

Building a budget for house construction

Once our digital plans were completed, we applied for a building permit through the city and started creating a budget for building our house. I also emailed various subcontractors to get free estimates. I usually started by selecting three different companies for each task. I always chose what best fit our budget (notice I'm not advocating for the cheapest estimate). Some things are worth paying a little bit more for, depending on the quality you want and what you can afford.

There is an age-old saying in construction: You have three options—fast, cheap, and good—but you can only have two, so pick wisely. If you are going for cheap and good, then be prepared for it not to be fast. If you want fast and cheap, then it is probably not going to be good. And if you want fast and good, it's most likely not going to be cheap.

Contractor or no contractor?

A contractor can prepare the construction budget. They will add a 15 percent to 20 percent fee to the total cost for managing the project, which begs the question of whether or not a contractor is necessary. Houston's building permit application asks for the contractor in charge of the project but there are no rules against simply writing "Self." But, a good contractor will come with lots of knowledge, vetted subcontractors, and an understanding of timing. They will know what to look for in terms of quality and will manage every aspect of getting the house built. Just as with any other person involved in this journey, they need to be trustworthy and reliable.

You can certainly be your own contractor whether it is a renovation, new construction, or addition—especially if you are self-financing and building as you have funds available. You just have to keep the building permit active by having some kind of activity every six months.[34] The question of whether or not to work with a contractor also depends on what you are building, for example a 5,000 sq. ft., three-story house or an 800 sq. ft. bungalow. Also, how much time do you have to dedicate to the project? Can you be on site every day? Can you meet people for price quotes? Do you have enough knowledge or experience to recognize a mistake? This is a reckoning of your abilities and being honest about the person you are.

Getting a residential construction loan

Once we had our plans, a researched estimate of how much the house would cost to build, and a contractor to work with if need be, we reached out to lenders to fund our construction.

A construction loan is a short term loan that is paid off at the end of the construction period, usually with a traditional mortgage, also known as a "permanent" or "financing" loan. Essentially, when you apply for a "one-time close" construction loan, you are applying to qualify for two loans at once. The amount you can borrow with a construction loan usually tops out at 80 percent of the appraised value of your future home. Construction loans are riskier from a lenders perspective since they are lending money based on a proposal. By qualifying for a one-time close construction loan, the final conversion to a permanent loan should be simple.

A construction loan can be used to either build a house, buy land and build a house on it, or to build an addition on an existing house. The loan amount is disbursed in installments called "draws" as building milestones are achieved, which are pre-determined by the builder or contractor on a "draw schedule." Construction loans are shorter term (twelve, eighteen, or twenty-four months usually) and may have a higher interest rate.

There are many types of lenders to approach about a construction loan:

- **Direct lenders:** commercial banks (local and national) or credit unions (local)
- **Mortgage brokers:** an intermediary who will shop your file around to various lenders (usually additional fees apply)
- **Private lenders:** friends, family, colleagues, or hard money lenders (investors)

The more traditional approach is borrowing from the bank with which you already have an account. But there are many banks and, even if you don't bank with them, they would be happy to sell you a construction loan. There are also credit unions and other loan agencies that offer residential construction loans.

Some lenders only handle construction loans, and some don't handle them at all, so be sure to do your research. Most lenders will know someone they can recommend since you will need a construction loan as well as a mortgage. Once the lender receives all your documents, they review the information, compose a loan application, and send it through an automated underwriting system (AUS). The AUS reviews the data and arrives at a logic-based loan decision. The system is a national database that collects statistics and data and will tell the lender if you will be approved or not and what is triggering the risk factor. A construction loan does require a bank-certified contractor for the job. The person you choose to become a contractor may have to submit their tax returns and list of previously completed projects to be approved as a project manager by the bank if they are not already on the lender's approved list.

If you don't want to deal with a bank, but don't want the project to drag on, you can approach a private lender. Since you will be borrowing money, you will need a contract that addresses the amount of interest to be paid (if applicable), payment and draw schedule, and repayment terms. Depending on the lender, they might not require an approved contractor and will let you manage the project yourself.

First attempt

I started our construction loan adventure with a lender I already knew personally. She worked with my parents on a home construction project many years ago and I felt comfortable with her. Our first attempt was applying for a loan for the industrial metal building.

Our budget was $186,000 and was based on a $30,000 down payment. Since we owned the land, we could use the equity as our downpayment. We separated the second floor build out, which got us to a final loan request of $127,000. The first attempt was intense. I received the intimidating list of documents I needed to send to the mortgage broker, along with my tax returns, authorization to pull my credit, and my last two bank account statements, which somehow felt the most violating since that is not something people typically see—exactly how I spent my money and how much was actually in my bank accounts. When Zak and I first approached the lender, we still had not purchased our property but were in negotiations. More than anything she was a confidant to guide us through purchasing the property and helped us get a foothold on how to build a house, what was needed, and what was involved in the process. Since we didn't have any civil or structural engineering plans, the bank kept pushing back, asking for more detail before moving forward with the loan application.

While we were living in the carriage house, we changed our plans from concrete slab to pier and beam once we learned about the floodplain requirements. Since the project changed, meaning the budget would change, it also completely altered what we were going to send to the bank. In a way, the plan for the grand metal building was a trial run.

Second attempt

While at the carriage house, Zak and I worked on getting our second set of plans (for the suburban house on stilts with modern layout) drawn and engineered through Jamie. I wanted to make sure this new layout was going to make it through the bank process but, unfortunately, that is not how banks work. They need to see the whole package in order to give an accurate answer. I spoke with Candice who explained to me the debt-to-income ratio and calculated how much money I would need to earn to build a house at a certain cost (or how much house I could afford with the income I had). This is what determined our square footage and budget.

Due to our Avenue CDC experience, Candice sent me the contact info for someone at the bank who deals with city grants and affordable housing projects. We learned that the grant could not be combined with a new construction, so she forwarded my information to a banker who handles construction loans. And then there were two lenders working on our house.

Third attempt

Our plans then changed again for the last time. We fired Jamie and my sister reconfigured the design of our house. With new design plans, we got

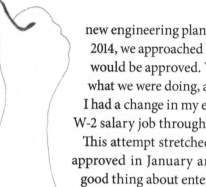

new engineering plans and created a new budget. In the fall of 2014, we approached lenders again; this time it seemed like we would be approved. We finally had a solid set of plans, knew what we were doing, and were familiar with the process. Also, I had a change in my employment status. I finally had a secure W-2 salary job through the online art magazine.

This attempt stretched into Spring 2015. Our plans had been approved in January and we were itching to get started. The good thing about entering a new year was that once I filed my taxes, I could drop the oldest tax return and use the most recent data (at this point, 2014 and 2013). It worked in our favor since I was progressively showing more income, leaving behind the finances from the years when I was a student, which made me more favorable to banks.

At this point, I had branched out and involved ten lenders. Each one essentially needed the same info so, once we had the package of information and supporting documents, we could shop around. I searched online for "construction lenders Texas" and frantically sent emails to companies that seemed like they would be able to help. As we were short on time, I just sent the same information to everyone, followed up, and provided additional details as needed.

Everyone wanted to help until they saw my file, then their enthusiasm diminished. I felt like a giant red flag, waving brightly. The reasons they gave for declining my application were multi-faceted: my student loan payment, the appraised value of the future home was too low, not having 10 percent of loan amount in the bank as contingency, and the average of my two incomes, neither of which had a long enough history and neither one enough for me to qualify. Lenders and underwriters need to see solid, slow, and steady growth with the same employer or within the same industry over the past two years. They do not want to see erratic income or expenses.

The student loan payment was really the toughest for everyone to wrap their head around. But, as many lenders said early on in the process, I wasn't the only one in this position. Banks and lenders want to see stable finances. Having a job, like adjunct teaching, that comes with an expiration date is not what they want to see. It is the same with student loans—with the federal Income-based Repayment Plan, the monthly payment amount is only guaranteed for one year, at which point borrowers have to recertify which makes the underwriters nervous. What if a borrower forgets to recertify and then has to pay the standard amount, which then causes them to default on a mortgage?

During most of Spring 2015, I was busy emailing financial paperwork to lenders and following up on the current status of the loan only to get a disappointing phone call telling me they couldn't approve my application, or they would send me a worksheet outlining that it would be approved if I brought $30,000 or more to the closing.

Red flag

I clearly remember one of those phone calls. I was walking around in our yard, dodging mosquitoes that flared up after the rain. I couldn't talk inside the container since the signal didn't really reach though the metal walls. It was hot and I could feel the sweat dripping down my back. The mortgage loan officer explained to me that he had done everything possible but he couldn't make any headway with the underwriters. Although he was affiliated with a bank, he had even gone out of his way to send my file to colleagues at other banks to see if they would have any luck. This was probably the third or so rejection within a few weeks and I felt stuck, frustrated, and angry. I remember listening, with my heart pounding, at a loss of words until I burst out: "But I'm not a bad person!" I think we were both shocked at that point, he not knowing what to say and me not sure how to best handle this moving forward. I decided to go with it: "I pay my taxes, I contribute to society, I am educated, I don't litter, I'm a good driver…" I was short of screaming, "What the hell do they want from me?" It had already been two years since first starting this process and everything had fallen into place except for this last major piece. Somehow I had accomplished everything people advised me to do but none of it was getting me anywhere and all of it was stressing me out.

He understood my frustration and said he was sorry he couldn't do more. Zak and I owned land, we had city-approved plans, I had a salaried job and still we couldn't get anything off the ground. The only way to move forward was to borrow the $30,000 we needed to qualify for the construction loan. We approached family, friends, associates—essentially looking for a private lender, pitching it as an investment opportunity. If someone loaned us the money, they would make more interest than if it just sat in a savings account. We couldn't get a traditional loan or borrow money on credit since that would show up on my credit report, adding to my already tight debt-to-income ratio. We needed something that wouldn't show up in the paperwork.

The proposition

Jim celebrates his birthday every year with a bang. Since it falls right around the winter solstice, he throws a big solstice party complete with live bands, barbeque, camp fires, lights, and alcohol. Although he had to take a little break between selling his home and buying the property, he was back at it in 2013, the first winter solstice after we each purchased our properties. It turned out to be a complete mud pit of an event. It rained all week and rained again during the party. We purchased crushed concrete to create somewhat of a stable driveway for everyone but the soil just turned into a soupy mess. We still did not have electricity, so we used generators and extension cables to power the lights and sound for the bands.

I had never been to any of Jim's previous parties, so I didn't realize what we were in for. It became a little clearer when, as I was washing dishes in our container the night before the big event, a bright fireball flashed across the yard. I looked up and there was Jim, in a thick overcoat, standing at what looked like a modified keyboard surrounded by fire. Pipes jutted out of the ground with little flames flickering at the top, each letting off a fireball corresponding to a certain key. He had set up his fireball pipe organ for the big event. What a sight! Surrounded in flames, all I could think was that I hope he doesn't set his beard on fire.

Probably 100 people came throughout the night of the solstice. Jim started the grill in the morning and prepared the traditional feast with ribs, sausage, brisket, and ham. There were potato salads, grilled vegetables, and coolers filled with beer, water, and sodas. Guests were encouraged to bring their rain boots and, although people were sinking into the mud, everyone had a great time. The band was set up on the pirate ship. We used hay to create walkways but, after enough traffic, it just sank into the ground. We cut down some trees where our future home was going to be built. Right around what is now our kitchen, we had a little campfire with logs set up around it. As the music was blaring, Zak and I visited with friends on the site of our future home.

It was at this solstice bash that Ed first came to the neighborhood. He was a long-time friend of Zak's father, friends with Jim, and has known Zak forever. His car

got stuck in the mud and he had to spend the night so
we could help him get out in the morning. He fell
in love with the area and, as we were trying to
get his car unstuck, he noticed that a property nearby was going up for auction.[35] He
inquired online, signed up, and walked into
the auction and paid what was owed in cash
with no competition.

He mimicked our set up and moved a 40
ft. and 20 ft. container on to his land. This is how we became neighbors
and how it came to be that he was working on his property when we were
knocking on all doors to ask for funds to build our house. Zak had the
uncomfortable task of walking over and making the ask. Ed asked how
much, in total, we needed for the house. When Zak told him $130,000, Ed
surprisingly proposed to loan us the whole amount for the construction
and he would get paid in full once we got our final mortgage. He saw the
investment opportunity.

The luck of all those stars aligning is still unfathomable to me—the
luck that we had plans ready to go, with a budget that we have pored over
and roughly knew what we would spend, and the luck of finding a private
lender willing to loan us the full amount. Obviously, we still had to figure
out how it all would work but it was something, a glimmer of hope that
this could still happen.

I immediately sprung into action, emailing or calling back all the lenders,
even the guy I had broken down with on the phone, and told them about
our new situation: a private lender was willing to loan us money for the
construction. The issue of the final mortgage still stood so we weren't completely out of the woods but the uncertainty of qualifying for a traditional
construction loan was gone.

I had been making headway with a Federal Housing Administration
(FHA) mortgage. Not all banks/lenders offer FHA products—it is a more
complicated process since it has to go through the federal government
bureaucracy in addition to the standard banking bureaucracy. It is specifically
offered so people with less income do not need as much money down; in the
end, though, monthly payments can be higher due to mortgage insurance
(PMI). When I contacted lenders again, many had either grown tired of
me, knowing that I was a waste of their time, or they saw the word FHA
and just left it there. Out of ten, one lender moved forward with me. I was

able to get a letter of approval for the loan amount, a good faith estimate that outlined the future mortgage with fees, what I needed to bring to the closing, and what our monthly mortgage payments would be.

The mechanics

Despite Ed and us being friends, we had to have a clear and concise contract in place outlining everyone's responsibility, timeline, financial draw schedule, etc. The contract also functioned as a legal document that the bank recognizes and can pay off with a mortgage.

Luckily, such a thing already exists and it is called a mechanic's lien. It puts a lien against your property and is usually implemented as a legal action by a subcontractor if they don't get paid. I searched online and found several mechanics lien sample agreements and contracts. I filled them out, tinkered with them, and discussed the terms with Ed. We realized we should have a legal professional look it over, so I reached out to somebody who handles real estate contracts. We discussed what we needed and he was able to pull everything together and file it with the title company. He also made sure we were protected and everything was fair. We settled on a contract with a time frame of eighteen months, an interest payment on the amount that had been drawn, plus a fee for Ed for his help during the construction process.

Before signing, I wanted to ensure that the payoff of a thirty-year mortgage would go smoothly, that I maintained my job and income, and that Zak could finish the house on time without a construction crew. I had to keep the budget balanced and make sure we could pay for everything with the draws we had scheduled. If any one of these things went off balance, we could lose our house, our land, and our dream. The advice I got from the mortgage lender was: Don't make less money, don't take on more debt, don't be late on current debt, and don't show a loss on my tax return.

The stakes were high but before long we were back in that beige room with the plush brown chairs and the title company officer diligently performed her page-flipping card trick once more. We would be back there in eighteen months. We crossed our fingers that all the numbers worked out and that we could get a functioning house erected on time.

CHAPTER NINE

Building

Building a house is essentially a marathon, a race against time, body, and mind. I'm not going to go into the details of how to best use a nail gun to attach two pieces of wood. Instead, I want to offer a kind of informational binder I had hoped the city would provide to help Zak and me through the process, essentially a basic outline of the things that need to be done in the order they should be addressed. I also want to emphasize that we received a total of $130,000 to build the house. We had a tight budget and needed to be conscious of materials—measure twice, cut once. Our only other income was what was left of my approximately $40,000 annual salary after expenses. We also had a deadline, a clock counting down eighteen months from the date we signed the mechanic's lien contract.

Certain things in the building process need to be done in a specific order but there are many ways to problem-solve, especially depending on plans and location. Sometimes things can be done simultaneously, other times it is necessary to fully complete and pass inspection before moving on to the next step. When building a house, site-specific problems need a site-specific solution.

Always have approved plans close at hand in case a city inspector decides to drop by and asks to see them. A picky inspector can bring your project to a grinding halt or you might get lucky and meet one who is easy to work with. It seemed most of the inspectors who were sent our way had seen plenty in their time. They were laid back, relaxed, more often than not just excited to talk to us about the house. They liked that they weren't just dealing with a builder or contractor but the owner who was doing it all. We weren't watching from the sidelines—this was our dwelling and we were doing the work it required. They shared some of their insight, gave us tips if they had any, shared cautionary tales if needed. When they told us stories we listened. Yes, we had plenty of work to do but this was also about building relationships. I think they often walk into hostile situations since their inspection could potentially ruin someone's schedule, and eventually their profit margin, if there is a delay. Sometimes the same inspector came by for various checkpoints; mostly, they enjoyed seeing our progress.

Before spending a dime, create a system to track expenses. In the beginning, it is easy to think you've got it all covered but, if you are not careful, the money will be gone before you know it. Zak and I used the classic shoebox method to collect everything. I sorted receipts based on category, added them up, and entered them in our original home budget spreadsheet in a new column with the header "Actual" right next to "Estimate." We tracked how much we were spending compared to what we had estimated. If something ended up costing more, we would see if we could make up the difference elsewhere. If not, it meant we had to put aside some of our own money knowing that, if we didn't, we would be short in the end. Unexpected costs will always arise. In addition to all the construction expenses, we also had to pay the monthly interest on the loan and our annual property taxes.

When we first created our budget, we decided on which tasks to tackle ourselves and which ones we could hire out; where we could save money on labor and which areas were not worth doing ourselves. These decisions were based on what Zak felt comfortable doing or had done before and knew that he did not want to do it again. It was a year-and-a-half filled with time management, budget review, and quality control. Our emotions ran the gamut from frustration to euphoria as our dreams slowly became a reality.

Utilities

As soon as our building plans were approved, we hooked up our utilities. We had already set up the electrical temporary pole—a tempered wood post with bracing, a minimum of 4 x 4 in. square, minimum of 15 ft. length with a minimum of 3 ft. in the ground. It sat in our front yard, ready to be hooked up, for quite awhile. This first step is already one that requires a special permit pulled by a master electrician. Once the electrical panel is set up on the t-pole, the electrician contacts the city permit office for an inspector to come out and review his/her work to ensure everything is safe for the utility company to hook up the live wire.[36]

In addition to Jim, we were blessed with many wise, old men who worked in a variety of trades—friends, acquaintances, or long time friends of Zak's father—who were willing to work with us. Our friend Lucius was a master electrician who set the t-pole for electricity. Once the t-pole was live, Lucius connected it to the 40 ft. container out front, and from there we connected an extension cord that wound its way back to our living quarters. We also hooked up a light in the front yard off the t-pole for security. It was the first electrical lamp on the site, ever. I believe we shed some tears when the light came on for the first time, its bright luminescence filling our front yard.

Setting up electricity seemed pretty simple. Everything was above ground with a line coming down from the main utility pole by the street to our humble t-pole, creating a series of connections through electrical junction boxes to ensure electricity is diverted in a safe manner. The water and sewer tap ended up being more complicated. Since our land had never been developed, it did not have any infrastructure. The GIMS map we needed to include when submitting our plans showed us where the city's main pipes were located. We hired a city-approved plumber since they had to open the street to create a t-off to our property from the main water pipe. The situation was the same for the sewer. At this point, phrases like "long tap" or "short tap" start to be thrown around and are important. A long tap refers to the city main pipe running along the other side of the street and a short tap refers to the pipe laid along your side of the street. Not surprisingly, a long tap will be more expensive to "tap" into but, essentially, we didn't have any choice since that's how Houston's infrastructure is organized. Sometimes in an undeveloped or non-residential area, there might not be any pipes because the city hasn't had a reason to extend the grid that way. Since much depends on location, it is a good idea to investigate a site thoroughly before building or purchasing property as these costs can add up quickly when you are on a budget.

The company hooking up our water laid a pipe to our plot, just past the front ditches, and we attached a water spigot. We finally had running water. With the crucial utilities for building (water and electricity) finally in place, we could move on to the next phase.

Grading and site preparation

Building has violent beginnings. The land is cleared, trees are cut down, dirt is moved and sculpted to fit the civil engineering plan until finally a concrete foundation is thrust deep into the earth. Every modern dwelling is a raping of the land. When considering the scale of our cities and the amount of people in need of housing, it seems irresponsible to allow sprawling homes. It seems reckless to allow the clearing of acres of land. It is as if we've forgotten how we breathe and what keeps us alive.

Our site plan shows a roughly 700 sq. ft. footprint in the middle of a one-half-acre plot of land. We removed some trees on our own but there were still towering large trees, 60 to 80 ft. tall, that we needed to take out. A short and stocky Guatemalan man came highly recommended. He came with two people, surprisingly only armed with chainsaws, ropes, and a ladder. No lifts, no heavy equipment. With bandanas wrapped around their foreheads, they looked like a group of Rambo impersonators.

They carefully planned their way to the top of the tree, then shimmied up using just a rope with the chainsaw dangling from their body, also secured by rope. At 80 ft. in the air, they tied one end of a rope to the limbs, dropping the other end to the ground, then swung the chainsaw around and started cutting off the limb, balancing using the pressure of their feet against the tree trunk. As the limb would start to crack, the rope was there to help guide the fall. And so they went, top to bottom, until they could cut the bottom of a clean tree trunk and use ropes to pull until the trunk was in free fall, hitting the dirt with a thump that vibrated the earth.

I hate the sight and sound of a tree falling. It seems like such a waste to cut down trees if the material isn't needed. Living in a flood prone area of the country, it makes sense to maintain trees, especially mature trees, since they help soak up the water. Clearing the land by removing trees that might be twenty or one hundred years old only to plant thin little twigs that might or might not live, all because they didn't grow according to our plan, is simply silly. It seems to me they should have seniority.

The crew cut down the bare minimum of trees necessary to build our house. Any tree that could have its roots killed by construction was also removed since trees falling on your house is not ideal. We had him leave the fallen tree trunks on the ground as it is much cheaper than hauling away the tree waste; Zak and Jim cut them up for firewood. The remaining tree stumps also had to be removed, including the root system, since we didn't want to build on top of a living tree. We rented a stump grinder to eradicate the root system of some of the smaller trees, systematically chopping them to bits, grinding them down to sawdust.

To grade the land, we used a theodolite, a surveying instrument, and rented a skid steer and a backhoe machine. We used the backhoe to remove some of the larger root systems that wound their way deep into the ground and to carve what would become our drainage ditch that wrapped around our house. We used the skid steer to smooth out the land and, with the help of the theodolite, sculpt it to the levels noted on our civil engineering plan. Our home site slopes slightly towards the drainage ditch which in turn slopes slightly towards the street. In a city like Houston, it is all about water flow. Keep the water flowing away from the house and then channel it into the city storm drain system.

Thankfully Zak knows how to operate heavy machinery but it seems just about anyone can rent equipment with no questions asked. Upon picking it up, you can (and should) ask for a quick demonstration of the controls. As with any heavy machinery there is usually a delivery charge which adds up unless you have a trailer with which you can pick it up. In our case, the machine rental location was not far away and we could drive it to our site.

The drainage ditch, or mote, around our house is not just a depression in the dirt. The water that collects outside our house, mainly rain water, is diverted through the mote back to the street where it collects into the city's storm drain system. Water should never run off to your neighbor's property. By enforcing less impervious cover on a property, the City of Houston also ensures that rain water is absorbed back into the ground which helps during floods and puts less strain on the storm drain system.

Our drainage system devised by the engineers called for an underground concrete holding chamber, known as a catch basin, which restricts the flow of water to the ditch through a set of pipes. At the end of our mote, just before the city's ditch, we had to submerge a 4 ft. cubed concrete box into the ground, a holding tank for excess water when it floods.

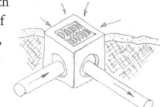

Foundation

With our land graded it was finally time to dig the foundation, one of the tasks we subcontracted. It was also one of the first large invoices we paid—almost half of our first draw of money from our loan—which was intended to cover grading, foundation, drainage, and water and sewer taps. Submitting that foundation payment was stressful. Not only were we paying a big sum but it also literally cemented our house in its location and shape. There was no going back.

Our foundation is pier and beam, with piers sunk 13 ft. into the ground with a 3 ft. bell at the bottom. The concrete company used a system of mason twine and levels to measure and mark our seventeen piers with an "X" on the ground. They operated a small machine with a large drill bit to carve each hole. The depth of our foundation (how deep the piers had to be drilled to hit solid ground) was determined by our geological test, or soil test. Once all the piers were finished, the drill bit was changed out with an attachment that created a bell shape at the bottom of each hole. Once all the holes were done, the crew added and secured compressed cardboard tubes over each hole which extended the concrete pier approximately 2 ft. above the ground, 81.3 ft. above sea level and 2 ft. above what the city required. We all took a day off to enjoy the momentous step of finally setting our foundation. For good luck, Zak and I threw a few coins into the four corners of the house before the concrete was poured.

The structural engineer came by to inspect the depth of the pier and signed off on the work before we could proceed. That afternoon the concrete truck got ramped up and the show got started. The truck sat in the driveway with a long arm extending out to reach each of the holes. One crew member guided the hose, holding tight as the machine spat out the freshly mixed concrete into the hole. As the truck started to pour, the crew placed pre-tied rebar in the holes and then used the remaining concrete to fill the holes.

The seventeen piers looked like a conceptual art piece: perfectly aligned, all of equal height, surrounded by uneven dirt. The mechanical within the natural. And with all the effort it had taken to get to this place, it looked so small, minor. It was truly just the tip of the iceberg.

I freaked out a little about the size of our footprint. Outlining something in a large area can make anything look small but the spaces between the piers of our house just seemed tiny. I went as far as even grabbing a rug that was stored in our 40 ft. container and laying it down between the piers on the dirt where our living room would be. It barely fit and there was nothing we could do. This was the start of constantly checking and rechecking the floor plan drawings and thinking, "Well, the couch does seem to fit" and "I know I measured it, so it must be O.K." It would be an endless struggle thinking about size and realizing the physicality of the monstrous task we had been working toward.

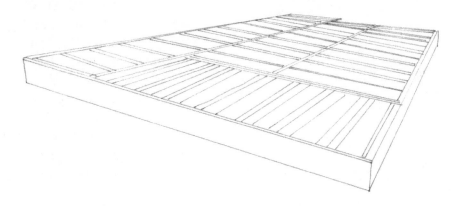

Framing

For a pier and beam construction, the beginning of the framing phase is more like an extension of the foundation. To create a solid base on top of the concrete piers to hold the house, we used laminated glulam timber, also known as LAM beams, a highly innovative stress-rated engineered beam comprised of wood laminations. The beams are secured and welded to steel plates that anchor them to the concrete piers. Between the thick beams spanning the piers, 1 x 12 in. planks are installed and secured with metal brackets securing them to the LAM beams. Together they make up the solid structure for the 1.5 in. thick subfloor, the base for the final flooring and the support for our two-story home.

The piers, beams, and subfloor are the foundation to start framing the house. Normally, this is another job that can be subcontracted to a crew of people who can frame a multi-story house within a few weeks but we decided to do it ourselves. This stage is important and should not be rushed since the underlying structure will affect everything from this point on.

Thus, our framing took a little longer since Jim and Zak framed the two-story, 1,280 sq. ft. house with two porches by themselves with some help. We did not save money on the foundation and we certainly didn't start

with the framing. Throughout the whole process, Jim kept saying something along the lines of "We are not framing a house, we are building a cabinet." They used 2 x 6 ft. studs on the exterior walls and 2 x 4 ft. studs for the interior walls. They carefully inspected, installed, measured, and leveled each stud before finally securing them in place. Living so close to the coast, hurricanes pose a real threat to structures. Our house is engineered to withstand 110 mph wind gusts, each beam secured with hurricane straps.[37]

Zak and Jim started with one of the tallest walls first, 20 ft., framing it out on the subfloor then hoisting it up and securing it in place. They built scaffolding on the subfloor to finish out the structure, placing two 4 ft. ladders on the top surface to install the window header box at the very top, 20 ft. in the air. Once these tall open areas were framed, they continued with framing the first floor, the walls now only 10 ft. high. Next they built the stairs and laid the trusses for the second floor. The addition of stairs was magical. Like a beetle that's just been staring at the ground, the open air staircase provided a new perspective, a new outlook. They laid the subfloor across the second floor, which provided an incredible view, especially since the neighborhood doesn't have many two-story houses. After work one night, with the second floor partially framed, walls illuminated in the LED work light, Zak held my hand and we danced across the subfloor. In the still breeze, we took a moment to count our blessings.

This all sounds very romantic and to be honest the building of the house and living in a container did not really put a dent in our relationship; if anything it brought us closer together. But the added stress certainly took its toll, especially when there wasn't room to give each other space. Many people didn't think we would make it past one month of living in the container without water and electricity. They thought for sure the lack of essentials would drive a giant wedge between us and we would be left living in an apartment, owning an undeveloped piece of land.

Instead, the constant need for reinvention to figure out how to live brought us closer together. The building phase was more stressful. All of a sudden we had money, a deadline, a budget to follow, and people to whom we were indebted. Living in the container was filled with internal stressors, things we could control; building became about external stressors. We had people asking us questions, rules we needed to follow, and the constant panic that we weren't working fast enough or forgot to do something, all of which can have an adverse effect on a relationship. But we had an immense amount of trust in each other, a trust that we would be there to support each other. He would build and I would take care of the finances, each of us playing to our strengths. We weren't married at this point, so nothing legally kept us together. Sure, we legally co-owned the property but if either of us decided to leave the other one would have been screwed.

The framing lasted into late fall of 2015, the rainy season in Houston. The surrounding construction site became a patchwork of wooden planks, mud pits, with white lye powder sprinkled throughout.[38] Since we didn't have a roof yet, the constant rain drenched the skeleton of our unfinished house, leaving puddles of water to collect on the subfloors. Zak drilled small holes into the subfloor to keep things draining and not damaging the wood. Due to weather conditions, our work stopped and our anxiety grew. There was still so much to do and soon we would only have twelve months left.

The deadline loomed large. We were counting on favors, people's extra time, and sometimes that caused delays. I certainly did not know how long things would take. I was used to working in a fast-paced environment where emails are fired off and problems are resolved quickly, almost effortlessly, while sitting at a desk. Physical labor takes a toll on a body and people get tired, they need breaks. When we first spoke with contractors, they gave us various timelines: twelve months, nine months, and even six months. Six months definitely seemed like a stretch—building a house that quickly doesn't seem to lend itself to a focus on quality. A timeline of eighteen months seemed reasonable for us, slightly longer than a seasoned contractor would need.

After framing the
second floor walls, we
installed beams for the ceiling.
The plans placed most of our heating,
ventilation, and air conditioning (HVAC)
mechanics into the attic but we realized the slanted
roof also gave us a good amount of additional square footage
in the attic for storage. At the highest point, the north-facing side,
the roof is 6 ft. tall. We laid down what we had left from the subfloor to
install the HVAC and still have space for storage.

Yolle helped frame the roof. To get the angle of the slant correct, we
tied a pink mason string from the front corner to the back corner of the
roof which made the triangulation visible. During the framing, he asked
whether or not we had a roof hatch. We hadn't really considered it and didn't
include one on our plans. However, we learned that a hatch is a good thing
to have, especially on a two-story house since otherwise we would always
need a long ladder to access the roof.

Getting dried in

Once the skeleton, or frame, was finished, it needed to be "skinned"
which involves installing 4 x 8 ft. sheets of plywood on the outside of the
frame. The sheathing is wrapped with a water- and tear-resistant material called Tyvek that protects the underlying structure of the house. But
before we could wrap and protect our house, the city had to inspect and
approve the pattern of the nails attach-
ing the plywood to the outside
of the studs. Once the house
was wrapped, it was time to
"get dried in," which meant
installing the windows and
doors. Using scaffolding and
suction cups, Zak and Jim
lifted and installed all the
windows, ranging in size
from 12 x 24 in. to 6 x 5 ft.

As we were now in the
thick of it, so to speak, we
really didn't have time to do

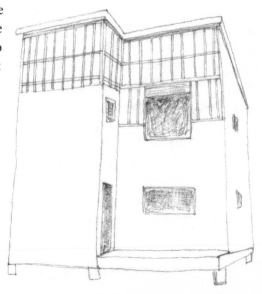

anything else. We dedicated every day to working on site; there was always something to be done. I worked my office job during the week, seeing the progress at night, but blocked out my weekends for whatever I could assist with. My mom decided to start bringing us lunch on Sundays—something small but much appreciated since that was one less thing for us to worry about. She would bring the food and hang out with us for a bit. It didn't take long before she wanted to help, so she and I spent a few hours every Sunday cleaning up the construction site, collecting nails, screws, sweeping the floor, picking up trash. Whatever needed doing, we did it.

Siding

The outside of our house is clad with horizontal slats of HardiePlank siding, a fiber-cement siding that is very durable and perfect for Houston's climate. Billed as a low-maintenance material, the cement board is also rot- and insect-resistant. The hired crew came with ladders and built their own scaffolding out of 2 x 4 ft. studs on the exterior of the house. They worked tirelessly all morning then, during their lunch break, crowded around a radio and listened to a soccer match. They continued working on site until the sun went down. All in all, installing the siding only took three days.

Roofing

After the siding was installed, the roof was attached. We opted for a standing seam metal roof since it is much more durable and, with a white or natural finish, it reflects the sun which keeps the attic and house cooler. We made every material choice for the house according to our budget but we also took the climate into consideration. The biggest stressors on a house in Houston are oppressive summer heat and the excessive tropical rainfall, so a metal roof seemed like the best solution. The roofers came and raised the roof in pieces, using ropes on the side of the house. The metal panels are connected by interlocking the raised standing seams together.

Once our house was fully protected from the elements, it was time to focus on getting the "guts," or the mechanics, in place, the things that make our house "run." It was pre-wired and then simply "plugged in" to the grid. At this stage we were not dependent on the weather anymore, which was good and bad since that meant we could work non-stop.

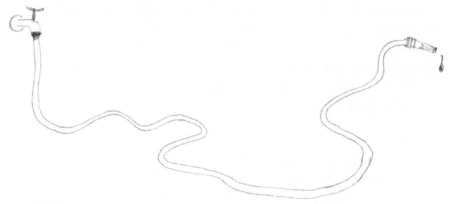

Flow

Although the architect and engineers marked all utilities on our blue-prints that we submitted to the city, we relied on the expertise of the master plumber and master electrician to layout the actual infrastructure. This meant things could change. For example, once we actually stood in our bathroom, we decided to move the toilet. We also changed the location of the return A/C to free up some space in a small closet.

The easiest way to explain how these utilities flow to and through a house is to start with water. Think of a standard garden hose spigot. In order to get water to another part of the yard, you connect a hose. When you turn on the spigot, water starts flowing through the hose and spills out the other end. To control the water, you connect a nozzle to the end of the hose with which you can stop or start the flow. You can then also restrict the flow for a pressurized jet stream or release it to generate a wide, gentle spray to soak your flowers. When you close the nozzle, the water stays charged inside the hose.

Essentially, this is what happens within any structure. In our case, the spigot is the city water main, and the hose is the plumbing that brings water to the house and diverts it to various points like sinks, toilets, showers, and yes, also garden hose bibs. The pipes carrying the water to the house and within our walls are always filled, like the hose that has the nozzle end closed. When we turn on a faucet, we are opening up that nozzle and releasing the water. All points of releasing water inside a home will also have a drain that connects to the main sewer pipe. These pipes run throughout the house, always set at a .25 percent slope to assist things flowing down (this is why the flush of a toilet is usually audible through the walls). The main sewer pipe guides waste water and sewage to drain into the city's sewer system, which then carries it to the water treatment plant. Once it is treated, effluent clean water is returned to the local rivers and streams.

I like to think of electricity in the same way, an element coursing through our house in the form of live wires. Similarly to water, the electricity gets connected to the city grid at the street from the electrical pole and then carried to our house via thick electrical cables. The main power enters through the electrical panel which then controls how the power is diverted to the various locations and how much power can be drawn from each particular circuit.

None of these systems were hooked up to the city grid until we passed inspection of their internal infrastructure. Zak was essentially everyone's assistant, the unpaid intern who did what he could to move things along: cutting pipe, gathering materials, drilling holes, etc. Since we saved on the installation by helping out, we were able to splurge and buy better quality materials. We have a Rinnai tankless water heater and PEX pipes (flexible plastic pipes). Everything outside our walls can be changed in the future with minimal effort; everything inside the walls and below ground cannot be changed, which is why we put most of our funds into quality products that would give us a solid functioning system upon which we could build.

All parts of the system—electrical outlets, switch boxes, pipes— are attached to or guided through the frame structure of our house, another reason to have a straight skeleton. For example, if the frame is crooked, the electrical boxes are also crooked, resulting in crooked outlets and switches. The electrician ran Romex wire after installing all receptacle boxes. Romex is a thick wire with a yellow outer jacket that holds the wires: a positive, a negative, and a ground wire. It travels from our electrical panel up toward the ceiling and then throughout the house, snaking through the ceiling trusses and dropping down the walls into the rooms, then threaded through each freshly drilled hole in the studs connecting the blue plastic electrical boxes. The wire travels until it reaches the electrical junction box then, leaving some excess available to work with, we cut off the wire. Every time the wire passes through a stud to get to the junction box, we installed a nail plate, a thin piece of metal on the front of the stud to protect the wire from any future damage (such as by a nail or screw driven into the wall).

Zak and I had a long discussion about height and placement of electrical outlets and switches. Now that we were in the space, and thought about placement of furniture, we could make last minute adjustments. Building codes requires an outlet every 12 ft., so people can comfortably plug in a lamp from various locations without an extension cord. Everything that requires electricity needs to be hooked up, not just electrical outlets but also ceiling lights, fans, and exhausts. Most of this was already noted on our electrical blueprints but things like switches or outlets—although dictated by code—were anticipatory. How much load per circuit did we need? Our electrician helped with these decisions.

Lucius came by on the weekends to help lay the infrastructure and give Zak instructions on next steps so they could continue the next weekend. Sometimes Lucius would stop by after work before heading home. If he had materials left over from one of his job sites, he would bring them along, helping us save on material costs. Thanks to another job he was working on, we found out that the City of Houston recently started requiring a conduit to be installed from the electrical panel to the attic to accommodate future solar panel installation (changes to the code happen and it might take failing an inspection to hear about them, which can delay you a few days until you remedy the situation). Working with us was extra work for Lucius and we wanted to pay him for his time but he refused. I think he liked sharing his knowledge, using his livelihood to help friends, and to have a place to hang out in the process. We made sure we always had plenty of food and drinks. When we made our budget, I joked with Zak that we should probably include a line item for beer since we'll be asking for a lot of help and free advice. It was the least we could do.

When we were almost at the completion point for laying all necessary electrical components for our house, we received terrible news: Lucius died suddenly. He had stopped by a week earlier to help finalize some things. We grilled fajitas and made tacos. It was a beautiful afternoon and we did not notice anything abnormal. He was a quiet, reserved, and thoughtful man. An avid golfer, he tried to play often. His grey shoulder-length hair was always kept in a ponytail, a baseball cap completing his look. He had a grey beard, kind eyes, and was always ready to help, approaching every task with a steady hand.

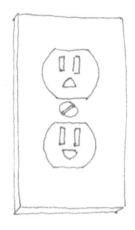

His death certainly left a hole. Zak couldn't walk into the house for a week because it reminded him of Lucius. Plus, we were left with an unfinished electrical system with the master electrician, knowledgeable about what went where and the system to the wire madness, now gone. Reluctantly, we had to start our search to find someone new. We were now operating on a short deadline, with remaining tasks piling up around Zak, and needed to hire out the work. A friend recommended Thor who had been doing some electrical work for him and could vouch for his work. His rates were not cheap but he was good and fast at his job. The story goes that as a teenager Thor was watching television at home and his dad was constantly bothering him about getting a job. Thor didn't really know what he wanted to do and one day his dad told him, "Well, you can't just wait for someone to show up and hand you a job!" Ironically, that is exactly what happened. An electrician working down the street needed some extra help and knocked on their door. Thor helped out, he liked the work, had a knack for it, and started working toward getting his certifications. He continued working at the company and eventually became the person in charge.

Before Thor could get started on our house, we first had to pay for a special test (not in our budget) on the existing wiring so they could understand what method was used to lay the wires since everything looked the same. Every electrician has their own way of doing things, a signature so to speak, which they needed to understand since it was past the point of completely starting over.

Plumbing is where planning for mechanical efficiency really paid off. All the pipes are primarily located within one area of our house, with the kitchen sink and dishwasher being the only outliers. Just like with the electrical wiring, every pipe horizontally crossing the stud needed a nail plate installed for protection. We have three sinks, two showers, two toilets, one clothes washer and one dishwasher that all need a water and sewer connection. For hot water, the cold water goes through our on-demand tankless water heater first before heading to the sink. The master plumber is also responsible for routing the gas safely through the house. Although we have natural gas which is generally cheaper than electricity, all points of access have availability to both systems.

Part of the plumbing rough-in inspection is a pressure test. Once all the pipes were installed, all drains in our house were plugged up using plastic stoppers. Zak dragged a garden hose up to the roof to fill the sewer vents from the top down (at this point the house was still not hooked up to the main sewer line) to test how watertight and secure the sewer system was in the house. Once we saw the water was filled to the top of the roof vents, it meant all pipes were filled with water. At this point, we hoped the drain plugs were really secured and wouldn't pop off due to the pressure, yet that is exactly what happened to Zak. The drain in the downstairs shower popped off which meant that all the water the entire system had been holding exploded out of the drain and into the framework of our bathroom. On the second test, everything held, thankfully. The inspector came to see the water level on the roof and inspected all the drains. Then we were approved—we successfully installed a sewer system that would not leak into our walls.

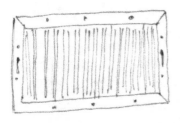

Similar to plumbing and electricity, the combined heating, ventilation, and air conditioning (HVAC) is another system of pipes, or rather vents. Silver reflective flexible tubes snake through ceilings and walls to connect the vents that blow out air. We opted for two units, one for each floor, each 1.5 tons which can cool approximately 600-900 sq. ft. They sit on an elevated platform on the side of the house to be above flood waters.

Our attic houses the natural gas furnaces and blowers, essentially our heaters and A/C fan. There are a series of pipes that provide natural drainage through the sewer for condensation the units might create. One pipe runs from the furnace unit to the exterior of the house. In case something goes wrong with the A/C, for example excessive condensation, the drip pan will overflow and the pipe at the exterior of the house will start to drip. The city stipulates that these pipes have to be installed above a window so we can see from inside the house if something is wrong. The drip will be an indicator of a major problem (obviously, we don't want water to build up in our attic) so we can turn off our A/C immediately and call an HVAC specialist.

The return air units, which suck in air through a filter, are usually

placed along the bottom of the wall and take up a
bit of wall space, almost a 2 x 2 ft. chamber. Our
HVAC sub-contractor suggested putting the
return air unit in the ceiling, which freed
up space on the first floor giving us a larger
closet in the downstairs bedroom.

Lastly, setting up our home communication network was interesting since
it is an industry that is quickly changing. Electrical or plumbing systems
have pretty much remained the same—there are better materials but struc-
turally the same physical properties still apply. Thinking about our phone
and cable infrastructure was the first time we had to think about what we
really needed from the house. Did we actually need a telephone landline?

After much back and forth, we opted to use a data cable and router instead
of laying a phone cable since phone service, even home phone service, is
increasingly converting to digital. A data box, installed near the electrical
panel, would be the hub for all data and communication. Since two data
providers had service in the area, we decided at the last minute to run regular
cable and the blue Cat5 cable, just in case. Like I said, it is always easier to
put things into the walls before having sheetrock to deal with.

Our mechanical rough-in was complete once everything that makes the
house function was connected: electrical, plumbing, data, and HVAC. By
this point, the interior of our house had taken on some color. The simple,
monotone, repetitive construction of the wood frame was now interrupted
and intersected with straight white lines running horizontally or vertically
for plumbing; yellow electrical Romex made their way like anxious squiggly
lines between the blue electrical junction boxes; thick flexible reflective silver
ductwork pushed on throughout the ceiling; and the blue and black data
cables snaked their way between the various points of input and output.
Our house was now fully wired. Before moving on to the next step, we took
copious amounts of pictures. We documented every wall, every major ceiling
thoroughfare, and similar because soon it would all be covered up. As the
years wear on and all this fades into a distant memory, it will be good to
have a record of where things are located.

After our mechanical rough-in passed inspection, we hooked up our
water and sewer. Electricity still had to wait until drywall was installed,
in case any damages occurred during installation. We did not bring the
utilities to the house in the beginning. Normally this is something that has
to be done right away, before even doing the foundation but, since we had

a pier and beam foundation and could access the underbelly of the house, we could wait to do all the piping.

Zak dug all the utility trenches—water, sewer, and electrical—using a backhoe, and the city laid the gas line from the main line to the house. As a precaution, the sewer pipe shouldn't be next to the water. Additionally, by nature of what the pipe is meant for, the sewer needs to be on a downward slope. The city's sewer infrastructure on our street is located about 8 ft. underground, more than deep enough to reach the extended depth of the lot. Our tap points ended up on opposite sides of the property since we had the 40 ft. container sitting right in line with where the utilities needed to be hooked up to the house. Where the water line is a straight shot back, the sewer dissects our front yard diagonally to bypass trees and our 40 ft. container. Always install access points on the sewer line for when cleaning is necessary; the general rule is every 50 ft. so that, in case the sewer gets clogged, there are multiple entry points.

Just like the drain pipes, the sewer trench has to be dug on a .25 percent slope leading from the house to the front ditch. Zak used a backhoe to dig the majority of the trench and used a shovel for the more refined parts, then he filled it with sand to create a solid base for the pipe to lie on to prevent it from cracking.

The city inspected all of our ditches and underground pipes before we closed them up to make sure everything was done according to code and nothing would cause any damage. One problem with construction in Houston, which has a long rainy season, is that the ditch might be dug and the pipe

laid when, out of the blue, a monsoon-like rainshower dumps several inches within a couple of hours. The ditch fills with water and mud and the inspector can't inspect the site to see if the pipes or conduit are resting on the ground because they are floating in water.

This is exactly what happened with our electrical ditch. CenterPoint Energy, Houston's utility provider, connects the electricity from the power pole at the street to houses for free. Since we are set so far back from the street though, that meant they would have had to install extra electrical poles on our land. It would have been an eyesore but free. Fortunately, since I was "Team Anti-Electrical Pole" on our property, there was a delay on their end due to a natural disaster and they didn't have enough people on hand to get someone out to our property; instead, we could pay for a rush service. At that point we really wanted and needed electricity, so we decided to put money towards digging a trench and putting a conduit underground for electrical and data. Zak used a backhoe to dig the trench but then, as the rains came and the trench kept filling up, the sides collapsed. Zak then went back to digging by hand, painstakingly shoveling the mud out of the ditch. It rained some more and we used a sump-pump to extract the water so we could keep working. Finally, the electrician came to lay the conduit and get things prepared for the city inspection. Once the inspection passed, we filled in the ditch and CenterPoint was back to a normal schedule. They brought the electricity down the main pole and threaded it through the conduit to bring it up to our house. We could finally tie into the grid.

Once our pipes and ditches passed inspection, we called a city-approved company to hook us into the main city sewer at the street level. The master plumber then hooked things up at the house. Even though we had utilities, it would still be awhile before we could finally have a flushing toilet. We first had to install insulation, sheetrock, and bathroom floor tiles.

Insulation
The main reason we used 2 x 6 ft. exterior construction is that it allowed for more insulation, those extra two inches adding crucial padding to the interior of the house to hold its temperature longer and provide more of a sound barrier. We hired a company to spray closed-cell insulation under the house, spray open-cell insulation in the attic, and install recycled, hypoallergenic bats (basically recycled rags) in our walls. The company provided us with some options and, true to form, we opted not for the cheapest, or the most expensive, but the middle of the road with good quality. We chose the bats, since they were cheaper and create a denser soundproof space. Insulation can be upgraded in the future but it is quite pricey. Because insulation is typically only installed on the exterior walls, we decided to order some extra insulation bats and placed them around

the bathrooms and inside the ceiling separating
the two bedrooms.

Sheetrock

The most transformational moment
of building our house was putting up
sheetrock because the inside started
to look like an actual house—no more
visible studs, wiring, or pipes. We hired
a crew of five or six people who came and sheet-
rocked our whole house in two days, using stilts
and building bridges to reach the ceiling. They left
openings where we would later install the switches,
outlets, and lights. They hung the sheetrock then
taped and floated it, meaning they taped together 4 x 8 ft. drywall sheets and
then spread drywall mud to make sure it had an even surface. Screwing in
the sheets can create some inconsistencies and the floating helps to ensure
smooth walls. It is a true art for someone to have a solid understanding of
how to float and to do it in an efficient manner.

To dispose of the sheetrock, we rented a construction trash container
from a rental company that picked it up when it was full (or when the
project is complete) and disposed of the debris. Up until this point in our
house construction, we had been able to dispose of most trash from the
construction site in our regular trash bin. We only ordered what we needed
and would rather go back for a second trip instead of ordering too much.
The cut wires and pipes were nominal and could go into the regular trash
or be scrapped at a recycling center. We didn't want to pay for a big trash
container so we were very conscious about the amount of trash that we were
accumulating. But since the crew was crafting perfect fitting drywall sheets
to our studs, there was a lot of waste, dust, and screws.

Sometimes the same company that installs the sheetrock will also have painting services. The cost for
hiring them to paint our whole house
with a primer ended up being
minimal for us and we had

them add orange peel texture to the walls, a surface that ends up being more forgiving than a smooth finish.

With the sheetrock hiding the guts of our house, the responsibility of creating the "look" and deciding on the finishing details now fell to us. Although we had our budget in place, I was constantly pricing out materials or researching kitchen layouts, essentially focusing on the interior design aspect. Up until this point, it had all been about raw materials; there isn't much of a selection process when it comes to a 2 x 4 ft. stud. At the end of the day, whether a house costs $200,000 or $800,000, regardless of the neighborhood, the materials used for the basic structure are usually the same.

In between the documentation of the construction process, the photo feed on my cell phone was littered with pictures of home designs and ideas for small spaces. I anxiously searched and saved things from the internet before going to bed, dreaming of the perfectly designed house with just the right amount of quirkiness—Pinterest-approved and totally Instagramma- ble, imagining the house that could be. I would see pictures of beautiful large dining tables only to walk through our construction site and realize that this would never be the place to house a table like that. Maybe in the future, maybe when we renovate. We weren't even done with the first phase and we were already discussing the second phase, how we could add on to and expand what we have.

I still had issues with the size of the house. Now with the skeleton enclosed, a boxed in space, it seemed even smaller. I kept thinking about our stuff being too big for the rooms. I kept telling myself that with the furniture it will probably look bigger. You can really drive yourself crazy—everything can balloon into a major decision if you let it. Even the door handles become a make or break statement piece to tie the whole house together. I felt like I always needed to be a step ahead of the game or I'd mess up and couldn't go back. This is the insanity of building your own house, because you can still make last minute changes until things are firmly locked down. Whichever way the gas line is brought in will determine where the stove goes. Once things are in place, changes cost extra. And so it goes on down the line.

I was constantly keeping a nagging sense of failure at bay. This is why it is dangerous to daydream yourself into a picture-perfect corner. You really have to live in the home before some of these needs present themselves. You will discover what you want, what fits, how you move through the space. You realize a house is meant to be lived in and your home gains character as it is used.

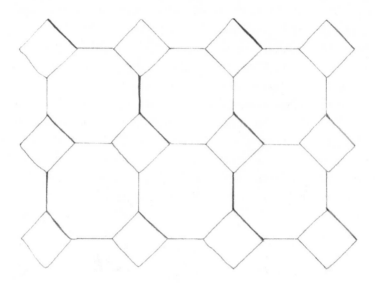

Tiling

The tiles were the first house accessory we needed to consider in terms of design. What kind of pattern did we want for our floor? Small tiles or large tiles? Does a small tile pattern really make a small room seem larger? How do the tiles fit together with the hardwood floor we picked out?

There are so many choices when it comes to the items that adorn the fixtures of a home. In many ways, our budgetary constraints made the decisions very easy. Usually there would only be one modern option in our price range but, as we searched discount stores and surplus places, the choices became overwhelming. The tile would inform the rest of the house. What was our color scheme? We decided to pick three or four overall colors, including the exterior of the house.

I'm not sure how many tile stores we visited but we finally found some fitting tiles at a place that carries an ever-changing array of discounted items in various quantities. We picked a green penny round tile for the shower downstairs, light blue square glass tiles for the upstairs master bath bathtub/shower, and classic white tiles for all bathroom and utility room floors.

Neither Zak nor I had ever done any tiling but we learned quickly since one of our top priorities was to have a flushing toilet and shower. As soon as the sheetrock and greenboard, a special type of fiberglass-based and moisture-resistant drywall, were installed, Zak went to work on tiling the downstairs bathroom floor. Thankfully, there is a plethora of online tutorials on how to do basically anything, especially new construction or home renovations. Smaller tiles do make a room look bigger but they require much more grout, leaving more space for mistakes. Grout can also be tinted which throws another design element to consider: How about white tiles and black grout? Because white grout starts to look dingy after extended use, and we knew we didn't want it for the floor, we opted for a medium grey grout on the floor and white for the wall tile.

The floor tile for our bathroom went in pretty smoothly and we finally had that flushing toilet. The shower was a different story. The green penny round tile we picked proved to be more difficult than expected. We installed it without problems but when we began the grouting process, things ended up looking differently. It appeared that the majority of the tiles had little divots that actually trapped the grout in the tile (no wonder they had been discontinued). Now we had dried grout on our tiles. I started chipping at it using a small scraper but considering the number of tiles I needed to scrape, it seemed unrealistic, especially when thinking about everything else we still needed to do over the next six months. After some consultation with a friend, I suited up in pants, long shirt, rubber boots, gloves, and safety goggles and tried an acid bath solution. Then I tried the acid bath again with a stronger concentration. Nothing. This was the beginning of almost a month of dealing with dried grout and figuring out how to get the shower to look good without having to rip everything out and retile it. I spent my weekends or afternoons scraping or using a nylon bristle brush drill attachment to mechanically remove the build up, all the while feeling deflated. If this was the way the whole interior of the house was going to go, we would never finish and everything would look like shit.

After the fourth weekend, I finally got the shower into a state we could live with. The mechanical process had removed some of the grout between the tiles which added to the messy look. A friend suggested to water down some grout mix and use my hands to fill in those problem areas—the goal was to have smooth grout with each tile somewhat exposed. There are still spots located in the corners where the brush couldn't reach that are a reminder of this hiccup. Even though it had seemed like a total defeat, each clean tile boosted our confidence.

Flooring

We had been eyeing a certain flooring store for a while because they often had good sales on their inventory. We ended up buying our floor—a blonde oak pre-engineered tongue and groove floating hardwood floor—much sooner than expected at $0.99 cents per square foot. Decent quality at the right price. We bought it, along with the padding, and stored it in our 40 ft. container until we were ready to install it. When the time finally came, we were in a hurry. We had purchased our appliances during a holiday sale and were coming up on the deadline for storing the items for free. We needed the floor and cabinets in place in order to have the appliances delivered.

Zak left for a quick trip to attend a surprise birthday party for his mother in St. Louis. Before he returned, he mentioned to his mom and stepfather that he was a bit nervous about how everything was going to work out. It was already the end of August, meaning it was crunch time to get things finished if we were to meet our deadline, and all of the remaining work really fell to him. It wasn't long after the birthday weekend that they hopped in their car and drove down to help us for a week.

They really hit the ground running. They finished tiling the upstairs bathroom floor and then moved on to the floating hardwood floor (which actually floats). It is a giant puzzle of wood slats hammered together and held in place only through the interlocking tongue and groove; none of the pieces are fastened down individually. We built the puzzle on top of the padding that sits directly on the subfloor, leaving approximately a quarter inch of space along the edges, giving the floor some wiggle room. With the table saw set up on one of the porches, Zak, his mom, stepfather, and daughter got to work. Someone picked out the wood slat that best fit the surrounding wood grain, another measured, the other cut, and then there was a runner to bring pieces back and forth. They started in the hallway, the smallest space, to partly test the system and get comfortable before moving on to the larger area. The system had all of us working feverishly for a week, cutting, knocking, and picking out fitting pieces until the floors were finished.

Trim

After we finished laying all the floor pieces, Zak went around and installed the trim. I never knew trim actually serves a purpose. In addition to helping hold the floor in place, it also acts as a decorative element, hiding imperfections at the edges of the walls. This applies to trim of all kinds—window trim, door trim, floor trim, and even crown molding. Since discovering this little tidbit of information, I have become weary of crown moulding because it might be dressing up a shabby sheetrock job.

Cabinets and counters

With the floor installed, we moved on to the kitchen cabinets. The kitchen took a long time to plan—drawn and redrawn from different angles, carefully thinking about sinks, sizes, widths, storage, and more. Our attached island juts out towards the refrigerator and we had to make sure there is enough space to comfortably still pass between the two. Each drawer has its purpose and they slide open with a sliver of room left. There wasn't really space for a pantry and we definitely could use more counter space. When we framed out the house, we realized there was approximately 3 ft. of untouched space underneath the stairs. I was obsessed with utilizing this space, finding ways to efficiently maximize it for storage, essentially expanding our kitchen. Rather than installing drawers or cabinets, as many people do, we left an opening to house a toolbox on wheels with a wooden top that would provide extra storage and could be wheeled out for extra countertop space.

For our cabinets, we picked a white glossy finish that would be easy to clean and stain-resistant. The countertops are solid hardwood. I really wanted a darker brown color for the countertop so we used tea and coffee grounds to stain the wood and create a chemical-free surface since we would be preparing and handling food on it.

Paint

I looked through many color samples and decided I really wanted a blue house. It was something different, something to contrast with the surrounding greenery. We settled on a blue house with white trim accents and a colored or wooden door. Siding paint for the HardiePlanks is best sprayed on, so we covered all our windows and doors with plastic. Zak, hanging off an extension ladder, sprayed the whole thing. We painted the accents (window trim, roof trim, etc.) using a roller or brush.

We also tackled the two coats of finish interior paint. We painted the ceilings "ceiling white" and opted for a light grey, almost white, for the walls. Usually one to stretch paint, I learned a lot about the time and patience it takes to paint walls. I was laying down paint, not rolling it on. There is a sound of sticky sweetness that happens as the roller kisses the wall with the wet coat of paint. First, I cut in the corners using a brush, laying down a thick coat. Since the ceiling is a different color than the walls and door trim, those cut-ins require a steady hand. I found it quite relaxing to just breathe as I pulled the paint brush at an angle across the point where wall meets ceiling rather than use painters tape. I filled in a nice solid border and then used a roller to paint the wall space, making sure to cover and protect the floor to prevent paint splashes from the roller. Similarly to almost every other trade, this step also requires lots of patience and awareness of your body, especially when painting the ceiling. Remember to take breaks—your neck will thank you.

Unforeseen circumstances

There are always last minute unforeseen and unsightly changes throughout the building process. For us, one of these was the placement of the main electrical panel, or breaker box. Usually it is in a closet, or behind a door, but it should be on an exterior wall to have a direct line to install the electrical meter on the outside. In order to figure out placement, it is helpful to have some sense of the interior layout.

Our panel was going to be into the utility room. It became the epicenter of our plumbing and electrical infrastructure. Because we had consolidated our plumbing, all the infrastructure converged around the walls of the utility room with the two bathrooms located next to it and above it. The gas also wound its way into the house at that location since the tankless hot water heater we installed was on the outside walls of the house, on the other side of the washer and dryer hookups.

With so much coming together and code regulations colliding with interior design decisions, that little room became a clustered madness. As our plans indicated, our east-facing wall was where we consolidated all of our mechanicals: A/C units, tankless water heater, gas and electrical meter but

all of these things have to be spaced out according to code.
With a length of only 30 ft., it was going to be a tight fit. Since
the water heater was on the other side of the exterior wall
with the stacked washer and dryer unit, we had problems
installing the electrical meter in the remaining 5 ft. to the
front corner of the house. The small utility room window
also became part of the problem, since the electrical panel
couldn't be installed under it as all the electrical lines feed
down from the ceiling at the point of the electrical main.
After much debate, we ended up moving the electrical
panel to the north facing wall which means we now have
the electrical meter on the street facing wall—not exactly
aesthetically pleasing. We also can't plant anything in that
area since the main sewer pipe comes into the house just

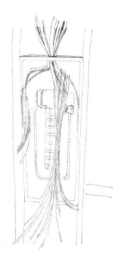

below the electrical meter. But, other than the electricity meter bubble on
the front facing wall, we really don't have any other tell-tale signs of this
work-around.

Final inspections

After we finished painting the walls, the electrician came back to do the
final touches by installing the hardware, such as light fixtures, outlets, and
switch covers. Similar to the sheetrock step, holes start to get covered up
and the guts become contained. No more wires spilling out.

The plumber came back to check all toilets, sinks, and showers. The
inspectors don't check if the appliances work but they do look at standard
built-ins in the bathrooms and confirm the kitchen sink is functioning. Final
touches for the HVAC system deal with vents of all kinds (bathroom vents,
kitchen exhaust, etc.), in addition to hooking up the A/C. For example, a
blower-door test is conducted to confirm the energy ratings set forth on the
plans and calculated in the beginning when submitting plans.

Once everything was hooked up, installed, and closed up, the final structural inspection consisted of making sure all the switches did what they are
supposed to do, that water came out when the faucet was turned on, the
hot water heater and A/C worked, and all the outlets functioned properly
and circuits didn't get overloaded. After passing this final inspection, it
was time for us to pop the champagne—we had successfully built a house!

CHAPTER TEN

Getting a Mortgage

In order to get our final mortgage we had to go through the same financial rigamarole one more time, this time sixty days before the end of construction. This meant we were two months away from our mechanics lien expiring and being contractually obligated to pay back our private loan in full. We were in a slightly better financial situation on paper at the end of 2016 versus 2014 or even 2015. In the eighteen months it took us to build our house, I had gotten a raise and started earning a commission on the advertising sales I was pulling in for the online art magazine. The eighteen months had also led to having another year of tax returns under my belt, giving me a solid two-year tax history with the same employer. Our neighborhood had started to change with new homes being built and sold. Low income housing was still being built through the city's housing initiative program but were listed at $180,000 to $200,000, instead of $150,000. Lots were starting to sell more frequently, earning more per square foot. I had anticipated these changes and told the banks about them almost two years ago—now there were actual numbers, verifiable facts to which we could point.

We signed the mechanics lien with Ed after confirming that we would be able to qualify for a mortgage once construction was finished. We planned to end up with an FHA mortgage for $140,000 due to the value of the house and my financial situation. As things were looking more favorable, and the neighborhood had improved slightly, Candice suggested we try one more time to see if we could qualify for a conventional mortgage. In the long run, it would be simpler, the process would be easier, and it would be cheaper.

So the lender madness started again. I contacted two lenders about a conventional loan; one we worked with for the mechanic's lien and another we felt comfortable enough to want to work with. That first lender, even though we had worked together in the beginning with nothing coming to fruition, ran the numbers with the value of our home and lot being conservatively appraised at $175,000. We could qualify but it was tight. If the value could hit a bit higher, we would have more wiggle room. After the estimated numbers gave us positive feedback, we sent the actual documents, updating our file which, at this point, was more than two years old. It just shows that even if someone rejects your application it's worth trying again. She had been very straightforward with me in the past and we trusted her. Between her and Candice, we were in good hands.

Since 2008, lots of legislation has passed to avoid another housing market crash, making for tighter regulations on banks. These heightened requirements standardize all applicants and force them through the same rigorous system. Electronic approval of an application is mandatory before it heads to the underwriters—who are real people—which ensures that no one will receive special treatment. But it also limits the lenders in what they can do for their clients. Anyone who falls outside the normal specs won't qualify for a conforming loan. Even if the mortgage banker wants to help and knows the applicant will make payments on time, understands the nuances of their banking history or business situation, the underwriters won't look at the file if they aren't pre-approved.

These standards make it difficult to approve anything even slightly out of the ordinary. The person is ignored—it all becomes about numbers. The process is black and white with no room for nuances. Risk management is key and, next to steady income, the determining factor is home value. The bank doesn't want to get stuck with a property they will end up sitting on, so they order an appraisal to assign a market value to the house were it to go up for sale or foreclosure. This is an important step as it also factors into determining equity.

Yielding a positive result is typical. For example, if you purchase a house for $100,000 and it is worth $150,000 according to an official appraisal, then you immediately have $50,000 in equity or assets.

Before 2008, mortgage bankers had a relationship with appraisal companies to conduct the valuations of homes, a situation that could go south very quickly. Banks could get in a routine, promise under-the-table kickbacks, or the client could make it worthwhile to the appraiser for putting a certain value on the paperwork. This seems like a Hollywood scenario but it could be something as simple as the bank or client sending extra information to the appraiser to take into consideration and skew their judgement. In essence, the new regulations protect the appraisers to do thoughtful, unobstructed, unbiased research into the area, current sales, and house value.

The process works like this: The appraiser will take a close look at the area and study recent sales of houses in the near vicinity known as "comps," or comparables. They usually stick to a close radius, zeroing in on one area but, sometimes, especially if the house is an anomaly in the area, they might go into similar neighborhoods to see how things compare and make adjustments as needed. In the end, they will select five properties they deem as comps and, based on their value per square footage, will determine the house's value.

So, even if someone builds a million-dollar house in a low-income neighborhood, it will most likely not be appraised or valued at that amount since the sales records don't support that valuation. It comes down to price per livable square footage. Yes, someone spent a fortune on that pool with hot-tub and added a media room with wet bar and bathroom, but it won't really matter in terms of an appraisal if there is nothing in the neighborhood to support what they spent on it. If homes in the neighborhood are valued at $80 per sq. ft., it doesn't matter if they spent $250 per sq. ft. The seller could list it for sale at any amount they like, but whoever wants to buy it with a bank loan is going to run into similar problems. No appraisal would substantiate the given value.

It might seem as if this little speed bump would keep values in check and prevent developers going into low-income neighborhoods and pricing out the residents. Enter townhomes and planned communities. The way to get around these regulations is to essentially build an army of comps that are all the same, with the same amenities, the same value. As they are all built by developers, the six or ten or more units will go up for sale gradually as they get finished and, since they are all listed for a similar price, the appraisers don't have to look far to get their comps.

Building your own house is one way to improve your neighborhood while not pricing out your neighbors because your house never goes up for sale. A lot of these values are based on the market which can be influenced and manipulated, similar to the stock market or art market. But whereas art is typically bought with expendable income and can be considered superfluous, not a necessity like shelter, the social impact from the market volatility is less severe. Not everyone has an art collection to play the auction game. Not everyone owns stocks. But everyone has, or should be able to have, a dwelling of their own. Even if you are renting, a rise in home values in your neighborhood could result in higher rent because of the increased property tax a landlord pays.

When the final round of financials came back positive for us, meaning that the numbers and debt-to-income ratio were approved by the algorithmic system, the bank still needed to order an appraisal to finalize the transaction. The comps included in our first appraisal based on plans for our construction loan were one story bungalows built in the 1950s. They had cracked foundations, were not elevated for floods, and had shingled roofs, but had three bedrooms or three bathrooms which apparently brings up the value. But they kept that first appraisal at a solid $140,000.[39] At this point,

our house was finished. We had passed our final city inspection, installed appliances, and placed what little we had stored away in the house—bed, dining table, etc. As this was right around Christmas, we also had a small Christmas tree illuminating our loft. There were certainly spots we still needed to paint and other finishing touches we needed to check off our never-ending to-do list.

The bank ordered the appraisal (for which we paid $450) and scheduled it for the morning of December 22, 2016. The bank couldn't give us any info ahead of the meeting. They advised us to show the appraiser the house and tell them about the construction but not in a way that would seem as if we were trying to influence their decision. As the car pulled into the driveway that morning, Zak and I were waiting on the steps to our front porch. To our surprise, two men came out, one older than the other but who definitely looked related. It turned out the son had taken over his father's appraisal business and, since it was the holidays, his father decided to join him on a few visits for old times' sake.

I was really nervous. These two people were essentially going to determine if we would pass or fail and, if we failed, there was no other option. But I took the familial connection as a good sign. After introductions, we walked them inside the house and through the kitchen, dining, and living areas. We explained that my sister drew the final plans for the house and that we, with the help of family and friends, built the house and knew it intimately. We explained the 2 x 6 in. wall construction, the type of insulation, and showed off the downstairs bedroom and bathroom. By the time we reached the back porch, we seemed to be getting along quite beautifully. The dad

commented that the porch almost felt like being at the beach, to
which my nervous self replied, laughing, "Yes, especially when it
floods!" Zak shot me a weird look and I could have kicked myself.
Who tells the appraisers that their property floods? And that when
it does, it really does feel like you are at the beach, presumably
because the water is so high!

I couldn't really think clearly after that and just kept nodding
along, trying to keep the commentary out of it. As we walked up
the stairs to the second floor, the dad made a comment about us
having to call the painters back to finish the stairs. And this time
I was ready—yup, we'll definitely have them come back next week
since they missed a few things. No reason to tell him that those painters
were Zak and me. As Zak kept the conversation dry and technical with the
son, the dad seemed to enjoy talking with me. By the time we reached the
loft, we all shared a laugh over the petite, thinly decorated Christmas tree
standing alone in the corner. But it gave them enough time to relax into
the railing and enjoy the view. The master bedroom, closet, and bathroom
were pretty straight forward. We also pulled down the attic stairs so they
could see the furnaces and insulation. The son went upstairs and, to our
great surprise, said, "Oh, you have a ton of storage space up here! Is that
figured into your total square footage?" Nope, it sure wasn't.

And that was that. As we walked them back outside, I mentioned again
that this had really been a labor of love from the get-go. Being lucky to find
the property, my sister drawing the plans, my mother-in-law putting in
the floors, Jim helping us frame the house—we really couldn't have done it
without any of them. And, as we stood in the same position in the driveway
as when they first arrived, the dad turned to me and said, "Sounds like it
was a true family affair." I just nodded and almost wanted to cry on his
shoulder. I don't know if he could see the desperation in my face but he
turned to his son and said "Well, we know all about that."

And with that, they left. And I had a stiff drink. It took weeks until we
found out about our valuation. It came in at $190,000—much higher than
anticipated, which gave us more equity and meant we didn't need mortgage
insurance. My debt-to-income ratio worked out beautifully and we were
able to add in more of the closing costs so that all we had to bring to our
closing was a check for $383.49.

Even though the appraisal came back favorably and all the paperwork
seemed to line up perfectly, we were still not out of the woods, and there

were less than thirty days until the mechanic's lien expired. The bank
needed this document and that tax return, then we endured radio silence
until they requested another flurry of documents.

The lender also had to pull my credit again, which meant we had to do
some maneuvering on our part. We remembered our Avenue CDC class
and how to distribute debt so we transferred our budget overages to a card
that was only in Zak's name. It ended up being a big bureaucratic circus.
We just had to go with it and wait out the non-responses.

Then the day finally came: we were closing on our mortgage for the
house. The same lady with whom we signed our mechanic's lien paperwork
at the title company guided us through this paperwork. Before I knew it, it
was over. Of course there is always some follow up, forgotten paperwork we
needed to send to complete the file. But gradually, the emails became fewer
and fewer. I was elated; having secured the loan, my newfound freedom
started to settle in.

Approximately one month after closing on our house, I received a final
email from our mortgage lender titled "additional structures." Not good.
Apparently our home loan was being sold to another bank.[40] This new bank
had started to look over our files and the floor plans and saw our shipping
containers which they wanted to make sure we were using for storage, and
that there was no water, electricity, or sewer going to either container which
would make them permanent livable additions. I filled out the survey and
added in the notes: "The containers do not have any of these things and are
not a livable extension of the house." Anymore.

Conclusion

With all of our mortgage paperwork complete, we finally got married in October of 2017. Situated in our backyard, our wedding was a celebration of our union but also of our accomplishments. We had lived in a 20 ft. shipping container without any electricity or running water. We had taken care of the land and sculpted it to our needs. We had built this house.

Many relics from our journey are still with us. The mercado market art car that Zak built with the elementary students became the arbor for our ceremony. We turned our bath house horse trough into an outdoor tub, a cool refuge during the summer months, which worked well filled with ice to chill drinks for our guests. We used the container, which became my studio, as a photo booth for the wedding. We turned a pathway we'd established over the years by walking to and fro into the aisle for our ceremony. It lead us past two towering oak trees that have come up strong and tall next to each other over the last 100 years. We said our vows under a tree canopy that we'd kept preserved throughout the planning and building process. Here, with the tree roots carving out their pathways deep below the earth, we had found our home.

As friends and family started arriving, filing into our backyard and exploring the house, the reality set in—we did it. It was familiar, it was intimate. It was the perfect ending to a journey that truly taught us how to build: a house, a life, a future.

Notes

1. A realtor can access and show you available houses in your price range and represent you while negotiating the complicated process of buying or selling real property (run comparables, do market analysis, etc.). The standard realtor commission in Texas is 6% of the home price which the seller pays— 3% for the seller's agent and 3% for the buyer's agent. If you use a realtor to find a rental property, the landlord pays 100% of the first month's rent in commission—50% to his/her listing agent and 50% to the renter's agent.

2. Sarnoff, Nancy. "Houston housing market continues its rise." *Houston Chronicle.* Last modified Jan. 16, 2013. Accessed March 29, 2019. https://www.houstonchronicle.com/ business/real-estate/article/Houston-housing-market-continues-its-rise-4196988.php

3. United States Census Bureau. "Characteristics of new housing," *United States Census Bureau.* Accessed March 29, 2019. https://www.census.gov/construction/chars/ highlights.html

4. German History in Documents and Images (GHDI). "Occupation and the Emergence of Two States (1945-1961): Currency Reform (June 20, 1948)." *German History in Documents and Images (GHDI).* Accessed March 29, 2019. http://germanhistorydocs. ghi-dc.org/sub_image.cfm?image_id=1018

5. United States Census Bureau. "Income of Families and Persons in the United States: 1950." *United States Census Bureau.* Published March 25, 1952. Accessed March 29, 2019. https://www.census.gov/library/publications/1952/demo/p60-009.html

6. Birken, Emily Guy. "This Is How Americans Spent Their Money in the 1950s." *Wise Bread.* Published Jan. 12, 2016. Accessed March 29, 2019. https://www.wisebread.com/ this-is-how-americans-spent-their-money-in-the-1950s

7. Rothman, Lily. "Putting the Rising Cost of College in Perspective." *Time.* Published Aug. 31, 2016. Accessed March 30, 2019. http://time.com/4472261/college-cost-history/

8. United States Census Bureau. "Historical Census of Housing Tables: Homeownership by Selected Demographic and Housing Characteristics." *United States Census*

Bureau. Last modified October 31, 2011. Accessed March 30, 2019. https://www.census.
gov/hhes/www/housing/census/historic/ownerchar.html

9. Noss, Amanda. "Household Income: 2013." *United States Census Bureau.* Published
Sept. 2014, accessed. March 30, 2019. https://www2.census.gov/library/publications/2014/
acs/acsbr13-02.pdf

10. Healey, James R. "Report: Average price of new cars hits record in August." *USA
Today.* Last modified Sept. 5, 2013. Accessed March 30, 2019. https://www.usatoday.com/
story/money/cars/2013/09/04/record-price-new-car-august/2761341/

11. United States Census Bureau. "Median and Average Sales Price of New homes Sold
in United States." *United States Census Bureau.* Published 2018. Accessed March 30, 2019.
https://www.census.gov/construction/nrs/pdf/uspriceann.pdf

12. College Board. "Trends in College Pricing, 2013," *College Board.* Published 2013.
Accessed March 30, 2019. https://trends.collegeboard.org/sites/default/files/college-pric-
ing-2013-full-report.pdf

13. Ibid.

14. Gabler, Neal. "The Secret Shame of Middle-Class Americans." *The Atlantic.*
Published May 2016. Accessed March 30, 2019. https://www.theatlantic.com/magazine/
archive/2016/05/my-secret-shame/476415/

15. Quart, Alissa. Squeezed: why our families can't afford America, (New York: Ecco,
2018), pg 147-63.

16. Jane Jacobs, *The Death and Life of Great American Cities,* (New York: Random
House, 1961), pg. 112-140.

17. World Population Review. "Houston, Texas population 2019." *World Population
Review.* Last modified 2017. Accessed March 29, 2019. http://worldpopulationreview.com/
us-cities/houston-population/

18. Many cargo shipping companies located near the Houston ship channel also operate container yards where they sell their recycled or retired shipping containers. The price
includes weather-proofing the structures.

19. Mayor Sylvester Turner. "No zoning letter." *The City of Houston Planning and
Development.* Effective Jan. 1, 2018. Accessed March 29, 2019, https://www.houstontx.gov/
planning/Forms/devregs/2018_no_zoning_letter.pdf

20. FindLaw. "Texas Homestead Law Overview." *FindLaw.* Accessed March 30, 2019.
https://statelaws.findlaw.com/texas-law/texas-homestead-law-overview.html

21. Maas, Jimmy. "Here's Why Property Taxes Are Higher In Texas." *KUT*

90.5. Published Aug. 17, 2017. Accessed March 30, 2019. http://www.kut.org/post/
heres-why-property-taxes-are-higher-texas

22. Ramsey, Ross. "Analysis: Property taxes in Texas are high. Don't expect the Legisla-
ture to change that." *The Texas Tribune.* Published Jan. 18, 2019. Accessed March 30, 2019.
https://www.texastribune.org/2019/01/18/property-taxes-texas-high-dont-expect-
legislature-to-change-that

23. The City of Houston. "Code of Ordinances, Supplement 84," *The City of Houston.*
Updated Nov. 9, 2018. Accessed March 30, 2019.
https://library.municode.com/tx/houston/codes/code_of_ordinances

24. The City of Houston. "Article IX. Building Standards," *The City of Houston.* Accessed March 29, 2019. https://library.municode.com/tx/houston/codes/
code_of_ordinances?nodeId=COOR_CH10BUNEPR_ARTIXBUST_DIV1GE_S10-317DE

25. HUD. "FY 2019 Income Limits Summary." *HUD.* Accessed March 29, 2019. https://
www.huduser.gov/portal/datasets/il/il2013/2013summary.odn

26. Intuit Turbo Blog. "Debt-to-Income Ratio: What You Need to Know for a Mortgage." *Intuit Turbo Blog.* Published Aug. 14, 2018. Accessed March 29, 2019. https://turbo.
intuit.com/blog/home-ownership/debt-to-income-ratio-for-mortgage-582/

27. Market Watch. "Student debt just hit $1.5 trillion." *Market Watch.* Pub-
lished May 12, 2018. Accessed March 29, 2019. https://www.marketwatch.com/story/
student-debt-just-hit-15-trillion-2018-05-08

28. Ivanova, Irina. "Why the housing shortage is set to get even worse." *CBS News.*
Published June 29, 2018. Accessed March 29, 2019. https://www.cbsnews.com/news/
housing-shortage-construction-worker-shortage-is-set-to-get-even-worse/

29. Lanza, Matt. "Houston's Tax Day flooding put into historical perspective." *Space
City Weather.* Published April 26, 2016. Accessed April 1, 2019. https://spacecityweather.
com/houstons-flooding-review/

30. RV Industry Association. "RV Shipments in March 2018," *RV Industry Association.*
Published March 2018. Accessed March 29, 2019. https://www.rvia.org/news-insights/
rv-shipments-march-2018

31. Houston Public Works and Houston Permitting Center. "City of Houston: Residential Permitting 101," *Houston Public Works.* Accessed March 29, 2019. https://edocs.
publicworks.houstontx.gov/documents/divisions/planning/enforcement/hpw_residen-
tial_permitting_101.pdf

32. The City of Houston. "Online Permits Website." *The City of Houston.* Accessed
March 29, 2019. https://houstonpermittingcenter.org/city-of-houston-permits/online-per-
mits.html

33. Mr. Money Mustache. "Getting Rich: From Zero to Hero in One Blog Post." *Mr. Money Mustache.* Published Feb. 22, 2013. Accessed March 29, 2019. http://www.mrmoneymustache.com/2013/02/22/getting-rich-from-zero-to-hero-in-one-blog-post/

34. You can do this by calling for an inspection or contacting the permit office and asking for an extension. If you don't have anything to be inspected and need to file an extension, there is a fee that will be assessed.

35. When a property owner can't afford to pay property taxes, or is deceased, the city can seize the land and put it up for sale in a tax auction to recoup some of the lost tax revenues. Even if it sells, the owner then usually still has two years to pay what they owe and retrieve their property. Tax auctions can be a great way to purchase land at a cheaper price if you have cash on hand, unless you have competition. You do have a two2 year holding period, but unless unknown heirs make themselves known and pay the delinquent taxes it is yours to keep.

36. Pulling permits—paying a fee to the city ahead of the work being done—is a major part of building a house. It also shows activity on the building permit project number. As long as the permitit is active, the structure could be under construction for many years.

37. Hurricane straps are metal plates, either straight (long and short) or bent at an angle. They usually have twelve or sixteen holes for nails that need to be filled. The point is to make sure every beam is secured to the next, essentially securing the complete structure down to the base to prevent parts of the home from flying away during a hurricane.

38. Lye, also known as sodium hydroxide, has many uses. Its unique quality is that is absorbs moisture, neutralizes odors, and acts as a stabilizers - —which is why its worked well on the soil yet wasn't harmful.

39. Since our first appraisal came back at $140,000, we could only get a construction loan in the amount of $112,000 (80% LTV). This meant we had to prove we had $28,000 in cash to make up the difference to cover our budget of $130,000 and the required contractor fee of $10,000.

40. This is common practice. Banks sell mortgages to either free up money for other borrowers or make money by earning a commission on the sale.

Appendix A

Debt-to-Income Ratio Exercise

Example 1: How much money should I make?

A person has a monthly student loan payment of $250 and credit card debt with a minimum payment total of $100. They want to buy a house worth $200,000. Can they afford it?

When starting with the home value, begin by calculating the mortgage (monthly mortgage payment, taxes, and insurance). The principle and interest payment (you can find various mortgage calculations online) on a 30-year mortgage of $200,000 at 4.5 percent interest (depends on the market) is $1,013. Let's assume this house is in Houston, Texas, and is located in a flood zone. It would cost approximately $4,518 in property taxes annually ($375 monthly), hazard insurance would be approximately $2,000 annually ($167 monthly), and flood insurance would be $700 annually ($60 monthly). The monthly house payments come to a total of $1,615. With student loans and credit card debt, the total monthly payment is $1,968. Since debt / salary = DTI, the equation is as follows:

$1,968/X = .43

To solve for "X" or the salary, divide $1,968 by .43, yielding $4,577, the minimum monthly gross salary amount necessary in order to afford a $200,000 house located in a flood zone in Houston, Texas. So, you would need to earn an annual salary of $55,000.

Example 2: How much payment can I afford?

You can also start by using your current salary to see how much house you can purchase. For example, let's say your monthly gross salary is $3,500 (annually $42,000), with the same $250 student loan payment and the $100 minimum payment on credit card debt. The equation is now this:

X/$3,500 = .43

To solve for "X," or debt, multiply your salary by .43 to arrive at the total amount of debt you can have which is $1,505. Subtracting your existing debt obligations of $350 leaves you with $1,155, the maximum amount your new house can cost on a monthly basis. This next step takes some trial and error to figure out the exact value. Essentially, you could afford a $140,000 loan since the principle and interest for a 30-year mortgage at 4.5 percent interest would cost $733, property taxes for a house outside the Hwy 610 loop in Houston would be a little lower at $258 per month, home insurance would be about $100 per month, and let's just keep flood the same at $60 per month. The total payment you can afford is $1,151, just barely below the $1,155 maximum.

Appendix B

Documents to apply for a construction loan

Personal information

- Excellent credit
- Driver's license and social security number
- Down payment (20 to 25 percent, if you already own the land it can be used as your down payment, also called "equity")
- Proof of income:
  - Most recent two years tax returns and W-2 information
  - Most recent 30-day pay stub (two for bi-monthly or one for monthly income)
  - 30-day pay stub
  - Most recent two months bank statements for all accounts
  - Current employment info (contact name and email address)
- Proof of income if you are self-employed*:
  - Most recent two years tax returns
  - Most recent three months bank statements for all accounts
  - Current profit and loss statement (often referred to as a P&L) for your company
- Proof of current rent or mortgage payment (factors in to your debt to income ratio)
- Student loan statement (a statement generated by the company administering your student loans that shows your monthly payments)

It is important to note that if you are self-employed, the lender takes an average of the last two years of business income as reported to the IRS.

Standard required project information

- Contract with a lender-approved contractor or builder: the person or company helping to build the house. They will either already be certified by the bank or will have to go through their own qualification process to ensure that they are reputable. The bank has the right to refuse to work with a contractor.

- Plans: includes site plan, floor plan, elevations, and electrical, structural, and civil plans
- Budget: customarily created by the builder or contractor. It will detail costs for all stages of the house, plus the contractor fee. Contractor/builder will also decide and submit a draw schedule, which delineates the predetermined building milestones that will correspond with usually four to six cash disbursements from the construction loan.
- Timeline for project: contractor or builder will provide you with an estimated timeframe for completing the project.
- Appraisal of future home: bank-conducted appraisal of your future home. The bank takes into consideration the neighborhood and similar homes that have sold and at what price, determining the value of your home based on square footage and the number of bedrooms and bathrooms. An additional (possibly required) appraisal is called an "as-improved" or "as-completed" appraisal.

Appendix C

Documents to apply for a residential single-family building permit in the City of Houston

- Residential Building Permit Application
- Plat Plan
- Geographic Information & Management Services (GIMS) map
- Geological Survey (Soil Test)
- Elevation Certificate
- Topographic Survey
- Plans (two sets)
  - Floor plans
  - Site plan
    - Note trees, sidewalks, driveway (material to be used), right-of-way
  - Electrical
  - Side elevations
- Structural and Civil Engineering Plan (2 sets)
- Energy Check (ResCheck)
- Grading Permit
  - Excavation and Fill Worksheet
- Wastewater Capacity Reservation Letter
  - Storm drainage application
  - Payment of impact fees
- Analysis of Impervious Cover Worksheet
- Deed restrictions form
  - Affidavit in support of application for City of Houston residential building permit
- Access Agreement for Construction and Maintenance
- Certificate of Appropriateness
- Residential Landscape Analysis Form

Appendix D

Our Budgets

Upfront Costs

Meals & Entertainment	$200
Soil Test	$300
Topographical survey	$600
Architect	$2,000
Structural and Civil Engineer	$4,500
Energy Check (Blower Door Test)	$600
Printing Fees	$100
Water and Wastewater Impact Fees	$1,950
Building Permit	$750
Total	$11,000

House Building Budget

Lot Prep	$2,000
Water and Sewer Tap	$6,300
Drainage	$3,000
Foundation	$8,500
Driveway	$600
Framing	$10,000
Hurricane Straps	$500
Trusses	$2,000
Subfloor Adhesive	$650
Tyvek wrap	$800
Siding (HardiePlank)	$6,700
Roof (metal, standing seam)	$6,600
Gutters	$600
Windows	$3,000
Window Tape	$250
Doors (exterior & interior)	$1,100

Attic Stairs... $500
Plumbing $4,500
Plumbing Fixtures (tankless water heater, toilets, sinks, etc.).. $3,850
Electrical... $4,700
Electrical Fixtures (lights, fans, floods, etc.) $3,000
Phone & Cable $1,000
HVAC.. $8,500
Insulation $5,000
Drywall..$7,500
Wood Floor $4,200
Tile $3,000
Trim..$1,500
Hardware (door handles, etc.) $1,000
Paint $3,000
Cabinets & Countertops...$9,000
Appliances..$4,800
Misc. Expenses (permits, trash, etc.)........................... $5,000

Subtotal... $122,650
Contingency...$7,350
Contractor Fee... $10,000
HOUSE TOTAL $140,000

Acknowledgements

Whenever someone asks me what it's like to be an artist in Houston, Texas, I usually respond with two words: "pretty great." Yes, we (still) have affordable studios and attainable opportunities from renowned organizations but the true greatness comes from the people in our community. They are approachable, accessible, and willing to help an idea come to fruition.

I would like thank my editor Nancy Zastudil for believing in me and jumping in with no questions asked. Many thanks to the City of Houston for supporting this endeavor to write and publish a book about building a house. I would also like to thank the Acres Homes community for the southern hospitality. Heartfelt thanks to Jim Settles for being the person you are. Joe Haden, we couldn't have done it without you. Thank you Candice Moody for your guidance and honesty; the same goes out to Melissa Kelly, Belinda Large, Brian Owens, and Scott Palermo.

I would also like to recognize the employees at the Houston Permitting Center who helped Zak and me understand the process; the city inspectors for being patient as we made our way to the final inspection; and the many people who offered their time and expertise.

The building of the house and writing of this book would have been a lot harder without emotional support from many friends. Thank you Kate Kendall for discussing and dissecting topics at length; Amy Yoshitsu and Emily Chambers for reading the beginnings of this book and providing crucial feedback; Rachel Hooper for your clarity and discerning eye; Daniela Antelo and Danica Badurina for your optimism as I made my way to the finish line.

None of this would have happened without Zachary Miano—thank you for always cheering me on and helping me believe in myself. My dearest thanks to my family for exposing me to the values that truly matter in life. Mom, thank you for teaching me to be brave and resourceful. Diana, thank you for drawing the home that resulted in all of this.

CPSIA information can be obtained
at www.ICGtesting.com
Printed in the USA
LVHW111931050919
629921LV00007BA/103/P

9 781733 054508